Worker Cooperatives in India

Timothy Kerswell • Surendra Pratap

Worker Cooperatives in India

palgrave
macmillan

Timothy Kerswell
Department of Government and
Public Administration
University of Macau
Taipa, Macao

Surendra Pratap
Center for Workers Education
New Delhi, Delhi, India

ISBN 978-981-13-0383-8 ISBN 978-981-13-0384-5 (eBook)
https://doi.org/10.1007/978-981-13-0384-5

Library of Congress Control Number: 2018948180

Cover credits: Jason Edwards/Getty Images

Printed on acid-free paper

This Palgrave Macmillan imprint is published by the registered company Springer Nature Singapore Pte Ltd.
The registered company address is: 152 Beach Road, #21-01/04 Gateway East, Singapore 189721, Singapore

Preface

We began this project inspired by some developments in India, which link to the future fortunes of the working class. The accelerated pace of urbanisation, the increasing precariousness of work, and the crisis of the Indian left are all key factors indicative of the growing power of capital. Against this, our project intends to intervene in debates about the appropriate response, and in particular, whether developing cooperatives or other collective ways of living and working, beginning within capitalism, is a viable path by exploring its successes and pitfalls.

In attempting this, we hope to enlighten the reader about the trade union cooperative movement an essential part of Indian labour history, and labour present. We hope to provoke a serious discussion about the nature and consequences of India's so-called 'informal sector', and of particular political responses to it. We also hope to provoke debate about the role of ideology and imperialism in helping to decide the efficacy and even the fate of workers institutions.

One of the most exciting parts of this research project were the places we travelled to and the people we met. The project took us all over India, to cities of Kolkata and Ahmedabad, to the hills of Dalli-Rajhara and the forests of Narmada and Gadchiroli. Much is made of India's immense diversity, and it is reflected in the different places we visited for this project.

However, a significant message to come out of our project is one of unity. All over India, we met workers and activists who are trying to change the world for the better, or who spent their lives trying to accomplish this. To observe their work, and to listen to their stories was a priceless experience.

The unity of purpose we found and the unity of the experiences of the working class in India was one of the great lessons of this project.

Entertaining was being shadowed and then interviewed by the Indian Intelligence Bureau when we were in Chhattisgarh (and having to explain where Macau is). Alternatively, we remember wading through a flooded industrial area in Kolkata to meet the Alcond workers and having Timothy's leg disappear into a muddy sinkhole as we walked along the road. If we provided nothing else, we were at least entertainment for the masses.

We are proud of this project and feel that this book is unique in some ways. It is the first attempt to discuss the histories and achievements of some fascinating social movements while in some cases also exploring the reasons for their decline. It is the first attempt at a serious critique of the Self Employed Women's Association, and a model of trade unionism and cooperative strategy we feel is based on a 'left' apologist understanding of globalisation under the influence of imperialism.

Included in this book are some case studies of cooperative or collective movements in India. Each chapter can be read as a standalone case, and we hope that fellow travellers who are interested in the organisations we have studied take an interest in the case studies. However, we feel that it is only by reading all of the chapters that a broader picture of various efforts within India's labour politics to build more cooperative and collective ways of living and working can be truly understood.

University of Macau
Taipa, Macao
Timothy Kerswell

Center for Workers Education
New Delhi, India
Surendra Pratap

Acknowledgements

We would like to acknowledge the contributions of some people without which this research project would not have been possible.

Firstly, we would like to thank Prerna Bakshi for travelling with us during this project and for providing her invaluable services as an interpreter. Having a professionally qualified interpreter with the necessary language pairs but also the knowledge of social science required to undertake this task involved a rare combination of skills, and Prerna was instrumental to this project. We thank her for the many long days and headaches she endured, and for her advice and guidance during the data collection process.

Secondly, we would like to thank some well-wishers who generously gave their time to facilitate contacts within the various organisations we studied, or whom themselves gave their time to participate in interviews and even to recruit research participants. While many people generously gave us their time, we would like to single out some individuals for their exceptional contributions. We would like to thank Ganesh Chaudhari and Janaklal Thakur of Chhattisgarh Mukti Morcha, Dr. Saibal Jana from Shaheed Hospital, Dr. Pradip Kar who introduced us to the Alcond workers, Bipul Pandya who facilitated contact with SEWA and generously guided us in our efforts to gain a better understanding of the Narmada forest region, and Jogesh Sondule who assisted with our research on Menda Lekha and accompanied us during the field visits.

We are grateful for the work of the editors and anonymous peer reviewers who helped us develop this work. Particular thanks to *The Journal of*

Labor and Society and *Geoforum* for permission to utilise our previously published research in this book.

Finally, we would like to thank the University of Macau for funding this project under the Multi-Year Research Grant MYRG2015-00131-FSS. The University's generous funding helped to make this project a lot easier. Timothy would like to thank William L Chan, Romina Abuan, Fatima Rogayan and Lisandra Fesalbon who acted as research assistants on this project. Thanks for your time, your effort and your friendship which helped to keep him sane while juggling so many projects.

Contents

CHAPTER 1

Introduction

The International capitalist system in the twenty-first century has entered in a systemic and structural crisis, and it appears to have entered a depressed continuum with almost no hope of recovery (Meszaros 2010; Foster 2014). With the expansion of capital on a global scale and with the increased integration of the global economy, any crisis of capital takes the shape of a world crisis. There remains no significant space to dilute the impacts of the crisis by shifting it to any other parts of the world, as imperialist capital able to do before the current phase of globalisation. In these situations, it appears that the threefold contradictions of capital system, the contradiction between production and control, production and consumption, and production and circulation, cannot be any more reconciled (Foster 2014).

It is in this context the capitalist system is confronting a closing circle and appears to be touching its absolute limits. On the other hand, by nature, the expansion of capital is a never-ending process, a question of life and death for capital and capitalism. It is in these conditions we have entered into what is potentially the deadliest phase of imperialism (Meszaros 2010; Foster 2014). The fact that financial economy has swollen to more than three times the size of the real economy reflects the severity of the crisis (Meszaros 2010, p. 28).

The contradiction between the limitless expansion of capital on the one hand, and capitalist expansion confronting a closing circle on the other create conditions wherein capitalist expansion emerges as a most destructive

T. Kerswell, S. Pratap, *Worker Cooperatives in India*,
https://doi.org/10.1007/978-981-13-0384-5_1

and uncontrollable process. In these situations, the more capital unlocks the powers of productivity, the more it must unleash the powers of destruction; and the more it extends the volume of production, the more it must bury everything under mountains of suffocating waste (Foster 2014). There is a widening gulf between production genuinely dedicated to meeting human needs and production devoted to the self-reproduction of capital, and it is intensifying the destructive potential of capitalist expansion. The impacts are reflected in planetary ecological crisis on the one hand and mass unemployment and the fundamental precariousness of labour on the other (Richard Antunes 2010, pp. 15–16).

Ecological crisis, mass unemployment and worsening conditions of work are leading to growing discontent of the working classes across the globe. Capital, incapable of resolving these problems, is unleashing severe repression on the people. It is also moving towards new and more efficient extra-economic strategies of social control, for example, surveillance capitalism; propaganda targeted to misinformation, control on media to control information, racism, national chauvinism, and creating and projecting terrorism as a fake common enemy to divert mass attention from these problems.

It is in this background; there is a revival of discussions and initiatives on alternative economies and, especially, cooperatives. There are broadly two types of such initiatives. One such discourse limits it within the framework of capitalism. This perspective sees cooperatives as a safety valve of capitalism regarding its demonstrative effect for creating an illusion among the working classes that there are still some spaces left in capitalism for prosperity. These initiatives are of a purely economic nature and are focused on the economic interests of only those individuals included in the particular cooperatives.

This imperialist strategy gets its reflection in the United Nations program on solidarity economies launched in collaboration with DESA (United Nations Department of Economic and Social Affairs), ECLAC (Economic Commission for Latin America and the Caribbean), ESCWA (Economic and Social Commission for Western Asia), FAO (Food and Agriculture Organization), ILO (International Labour Organization), OECD (Organisation for Economic Co-operation and Development), TDR (Special Programme for Research and Training in Tropical Diseases), UN Women (United Nations Entity for Gender Equality and the Empowerment of Women), UNAIDS (Joint United Nations Programme on HIV/AIDS), UNCTAD (United Nations Conference on Trade and Development), UNDP (United Nations Development Programme), UNECE (United Nations Economic Commission for Europe), UNEP (United Nations Environment Programme), UNESCO (United Nations Organization for Education Science and Culture), UNIDO (United Nations Industrial Development Organization), UN-NGLS (United Nations Non-Governmental Liaison Service), UNRISD (United Nations Research Institute for Social Development), WFP (World Food Programme) and WHO (World Health Organization) (TFSSE 2014).

There are scores of such initiatives at the ground level in various countries which are co-opted, supported and funded by the above institutions and various other imperialist funding agencies. On the national scale, this strategy is most widely practised in Brazil and, as a result, receives considerable space in the conceptual frameworks of the World Social Forum (Kerswell 2012). In India, the Self-Employed Women's Association (SEWA) is the most prominent example working on pro-capitalist cooperative strategies on a broader scale.

The primary objective of the United Nations solidarity economy program is a claim to help achieve the so-called millennium development goals (MDG). These include the transition from an informal sector to decent work, the greening of the economy and society, sustainable cities and human settlements, women's well-being and empowerment, local economic development, food security and smallholder empowerment, universal health coverage, and transformative finance (ibid). In practice, this strategy helps only a few individual workers to survive at a bare minimum level. However, this is widely propagated and projected as a viable alternative within a capitalist framework, for the sole motive of creating an illusion and watering down the growing discontents among the working class.

The alternative discourse targets the transcending of capital and capitalism. Such movements emerge as a political, economic, social and cultural movement rather than a purely economic movement. As Meszaros proposed in his book *Beyond Capital*, we can launch the fight against the logic of capital, and win famous battles "within the formal institutional domains of a capitalist society itself, making the actualization of revolutionary socialist politics—a genuine movement toward socialism—strategically viable within capitalist boundaries" (Foster 2014). However, this can only work if there is "a wholesale struggle against all aspects of the capital relation and the progressive substitution of an alternative organic mode of social control within the pores of the current society" (Mészáros 1995; Foster 2014). Thus, the class struggle between labour and capital is being carried out in all spheres of life, and labour needs to pursue this goal consciously.

The basic task of the working class movement is challenging and fighting the domination of capital in all spheres of life and projecting and creating socialist alternatives. Without setting alternative collective institutions in social, cultural, political and economic spheres and without the presence of a consistent struggle for these, it is hard to develop and retain a collective and socialist consciousness in the working classes (Kerswell and Pratap 2017). It is in this context that creating institutions which promote collective ways of living and working gain significance for the working class. These institutions also serve as social laboratories for devising democratic strategies providing better space towards resolving various social problems and social contradictions among working classes based on religion, gender and caste divisions.

The most all-out ideological offensive of capital in the present era of imperialism is the triumphalist view that 'there is no alternative to capitalism'. The presence of alternatives creates hope, and the absence of alternatives creates pessimism among the working classes. It is in this light in the current era without a broad socialist bloc, the task of creating alternative collective institutions in the social, cultural, political and economic spheres gains added relevance for the working class movement. Highlighting the demonstrative significance of cooperatives, Marx said, "Its great merit is to practically show that the present pauperising and despotic system of the subordination of labour to capital can be superseded by the Republican and beneficent system of the association of free and equal producers" (Marx and Engels 1976, p. 81).

This perspective is reflected in various initiatives of the working class movement across the globe in building collective and cooperative institutions as a strategy of working-class movement towards transcending the capital. The most prominent example is that of Venezuela which has been studied by Ciccariello-Maher (2016) in the book *Building the Commune*. In India, the most prominently discussed example is Chhattisgarh Mukti Morcha which is a central subject of study in this book.

The present study critically analyses the transformative potential of various aspects of cooperative movements in India by situating them in the above conceptual framework. We base this study on interviews with workers and members and office bearers of trade unions, cooperatives and peoples' organisations. It centres on four social experiments: (a) the cooperative initiatives of Chhattisgarh Mines Shramik Sangh in and around Dalli-Rajhara, Chhattisgarh, (b) collective institutions created by a people's initiative in Menda, Maharashtra, (c) an industrial worker's cooperative run by the

Centre for Indian Trade Unions (CITU) in Kolkata, and (d) a construction workers cooperative run by SEWA in Ahmedabad, Gujarat.

The study is the result of lengthy field work which took place in the summer of 2015. The researchers visited various sites in India conducting field observations and interviews, including Dalli-Rajhara and Raipur in Chhattisgarh, Kolkata in West Bengal, Ahmedabad and the Narmada district of Gujarat, and Gadchiroli in Maharashtra. In all, we interviewed over 200 workers, farmers, members and office bearers of unions, cooperatives, and peoples organisations, and political leaders as part of this study. Interview participants were selected via both purposive and snowball sampling. The researchers established contact with key leaders or informants within each movement and were able to gain access to a wider range of interviews as a result. As noted by Cresswell (2005, p. 203) "the intent is not to generalize to a population, but to develop an in-depth exploration of a central phenomenon", in this case, the experience of being part of the cooperative movements of workers discussed in the various cases of this book. A random sampling approach would not be appropriate in this context. Rather than generalizing our results as a representative sample of each case, our goal was to learn as much as possible from those with vast experience with the movement, in other words, from people who were rich in information, and in particular from people who were key decision makers.

The overall purpose of this work is to consider what role if any cooperatives could play in transformative politics, particularly in countries like India which have significant labour surpluses and a large informal sector. This discussion necessitates a critical examination of the concept of the informal economy and its application in India. The first chapter, considering India's informal sector, is raising questions about the utilisation of this concept in the academic, activist and policy literature. We demystify the idea of the informal economy in India, revealing the multilayered existence of various groups of workers in vulnerable positions which are by no means inevitable or permanent but instead are the product of India's history and political economy.

Specific interventions, such as the formation of workers cooperatives, have the potential to transform the lives of India's unorganised workers, but any intervention would need to target the specific requirements of each group of unorganised workers. We argue that the concept and discourse of the informal sectors imply the permanence of unorganised, unregulated work. Conceptualising Indian labour in this way leads to a position that the state should provide support and welfare measures to help workers survive at a bare minimum level of subsistence, but also to a fundamental failure to address the structural and specific causes of vulnerabilities.

The subsequent chapters consider various aspects of the cooperative movement in India, primarily when the cooperative movement has had some interaction with the trade union movement in some form. The case studies selected represent different kinds of worker cooperatives with different histories and ideologies involved in their creation. They have been chosen to present a broad picture of the Indian cooperative worker's movement and to highlight the strengths and weaknesses of particular strategies and tactics from the perspective of the working class.

Chapter 3 presents the historical emergence of Chhattisgarh Mukti Morcha (CMM), its path-breaking experiments and achievements regarding initiating various collective and cooperative institutions including mines cooperatives, a hospital, some schools, a cooperative garage and also a farming cooperative. The study presents the dynamics of these cooperative-collective institutions, their linkage with the mass movement and their transformative potential regarding transcending the capital. The study also critically analyses the ideological, political strengths and weaknesses linked to the significant achievements and considerable limitations of the movement and also responsible for the downfall of the movement. The union's decline is not an inevitable result of globalisation, we argue, but the result of individual fundamental weaknesses in the leadership structure of the union, and some of its strategy and tactics.

CMM built a powerful cooperative movement with an influence well beyond industrial unionism. The movement's concept was revolutionary in India and marked the first time a trade union went beyond industrial concerns. CMM advocated for 24/7 unionism, the idea that the union should be an essential part of the workers' lives always, as a model for unions in general, but mainly when organising contract labourers.

We will argue that despite these achievements, the union faced vital problems. Some inbuilt weaknesses in its work contributed to an inability to respond to these problems and its eventual decline. Nonetheless, the history of CMM is a case study in the possibilities that cooperative formation presents, but also the contradictions that can emerge from a new and innovative type of unionism.

An essential part of the dynamics involved in the creation of the informal sector is the generation of surplus labour from rural areas, in particular through rising input costs of farming, and the mechanisation of agriculture. Since the onset of its liberalisation policy framework in 1994, India's workers and peasants have faced a rapidly deteriorating situation. Various policy prescriptions from neoliberalism to orthodox Marxism suggest that there are no alternatives to capitalistic development and therefore the proletarianization and urbanisation of India's population. These policy prescriptions have generated crises in employment and agriculture, as well as avoid in alternatives.

Chapter 4 presents the case study of the Alcond Employees Industrial Co-Operative Society Ltd. (Alcond Cooperative henceforth), a wire factory owned and run by workers in Kolkata, West Bengal, India. The Alcond Cooperative is an industrial cooperative, in that the workers manage a capital-intensive production process. The Alcond case is therefore necessary. From this case, we hope to learn lessons about the formation of industrial cooperatives and their unique challenges. This cooperative is run by workers affiliated to Center of Indian Trade Unions (CITU), the trade union wing of Communist Party of India (Marxist) (CPIM henceforth). The cooperative is currently facing a grave crisis of survival. Along with other factors related to politics and economics of liberalisation, the limitations and challenges of this cooperative also appear to be interlinked with ideological and political problems of the CPIM.

To ground our analysis of the Alcond Cooperative in its local context, we will also discuss the specific nature of the economic conditions of West Bengal. We will present a brief overview of the economic structure of West Bengal as well as a discussion of capital flight as a critical trend that impacted the province and helped generate a process of cooperative formation. We will also discuss the history and ideology of the Communist Party of India (Marxist) (CPIM henceforth), the political party that governed the province from 1977 to 2011 and was the most extended democratically elected Marxist provincial governments in the world. The CPIM played a significant role in the Alcond Cooperative's history, not just as the governing party, but by forming, initiating and running the Alcond Cooperative through the Centre for Indian Trade Unions (CITU henceforth), the trade union arm of the CPIM.

We will discuss the history of the Alcond Cooperative, including its formation and management. In this section, we will consider the structure of the organisation and how it makes decisions. We will also discuss the technical aspects of the Alcond Cooperative's work, what types of materials the factory produces, and where the factory sits in the overall structure of production in India. Finally, in this section, we will consider the impact of cooperative formation on the pay and conditions of Alcond Cooperative's workers.

The chapter will conclude with a statement of the lessons that we can learn from the Alcond cooperative. The Alcond Cooperative should be celebrated as an example of how workers can own and run a factory that produces highly technical materials and relatively capital-intensive processes. The case did, however, demonstrate some weaknesses, some objective and some subjective. Regarding the material weaknesses of industrial cooperatives, they appear to be the result of the merging of industrial and financial capital. The Alcond Cooperative found itself progressively frozen out of the financial system and dependent on political favours and its skills base to maintain itself. This problem would be likely to replicate itself in many situations where workers have the necessary skills but not the necessary capital. This is a significant question that the trade union movement would need to think through to address this problem with industrial cooperatives.

Chapter 5 presents the study on SEWA Rachaita construction workers cooperative run by Self-Employed Women's Association of India (SEWA) in Ahmedabad, Gujarat. SEWA is almost universally praised for its work in organising women in India's informal sector but has never been examined from a critical perspective. It is an important organisation with a growing membership in India, and a growing presence globally with newly gained influence in the International Trade Union Confederation, foundations like Women in Informal Employment Globalizing and Organising (WIEGO) and with sister organisations being created in other countries similar to India. In this study, we critically assess the SEWA movement both regarding its big-picture strategy, and the grassroots of its movement. We find that the strategies and tactics employed by SEWA expose the Indian working class to significant imperialist intervention through donations by highly politicised groups which have given these groups significant leverage over the organisation.

The study demonstrates the dynamics of SEWA's Rachaita Construction Cooperative and challenges that it is facing. Far from significantly improving the wages and working conditions of women workers, the cooperative appears to the leverage the social prestige of the SEWA organisation, including amongst its members, to deliver pay and conditions which are weak even by capitalistic labour market standards. A purely economic enterprise, the transformative potential appears to be highly limited, and this aspect is not reflected in its theory and practice. Moreover, after many years of work, the cooperative is still not self-sustainable and still partly dependent on financial support from outside. SEWA's ideological and political problems link with the problems of this co-op.

SEWA institutions contribute to a de-radicalisation of the Indian working class, as well as a de-radicalisation of Indian working women in gender politics. We will argue that SEWA as an organisation is a product of hegemonic forms of imperialism, both in the trade union imperialism discussed by Scipes (2010a, b) as well as hegemonic imperialism from the US government itself. We see SEWA's rise to significance in the spread of SEWA to various parts of India, but also importantly, to different countries in the global South and on the international stage in the UN apparatus and the international trade union movement.

Chapter 6, presents a study of Menda people's initiatives to create various collective and cooperative institutions at the village level to promote a collective way of living and working and to transform the lives of the people. The Menda village is in Gadchiroli, Maharashtra and this is one of the very few forest villages able to materialise their rights to control over their forest and forest produce under Forest Rights Act 2006. The study demonstrates how the village leaders capitalised on a wave of politicisation around an anti-dam movement, to transform the village and its structures of ownership and social relations. In doing so, they created an efficient model of resistance against the mainstream policies of development.

Menda appears to be most dynamic social movement at the village level, with its highly significant achievements regarding building collective dynamics in production as well as social life of villagers. However, due to the rigid boundaries of work at the village level, it has not been able to theorise its experiences by situating it in the national context and therefore has not been able to formulate any consistent strategy of social change. This problem also gets reflected in the lack of ideological and political education of the people who are drivers of change.

The concluding chapter summarises the experiences of the various social movements as discussed in earlier chapters, their achievements, setbacks and challenges regarding their transformative potential towards transcending capital and capitalism. While keeping the different historical specificities of these movements in mind, there are still lessons to be learned from each of these experiences. The cases presented in this book deliver valuable insights into apolitical ideology, political strategy and Indian politics and of course into the practical difficulties of cooperative formation as a strategy to enhance the lives of working-class people.

References

Ciccariello-Maher, George. 2016. *Building the Commune*. London: Verso.

Creswell, J. W. 2005. *Educational Research: Planning, Conducting, and Evaluating Quantitative and Qualitative Research* (2nd Edition). Upper Saddle River, NJ: Merrill.

Foster, J. B. 2014. Mészáros and the Critique of the Capital System: Foreword to the Necessity of Social Control. *Monthly Review*, Vol 66, Iss 07 (December).

Kerswell, Timothy and Pratap, Surendra. 2017. Some Reflections on Crisis of Left in India. *Marxism21*. Vol 14, Iss 1. P366.

Kerswell, Timothy. 2012. Globalizing the Social Movements? Labor and the World Social Forum. *Theory in Action*. Vol 5, Iss 3. 73–92

Marx, K and Engels, F. 1976. *Selected Works, Volume One*. Moscow: Progress Publishers.

Mészáros, István. 1995. *Beyond Capital: Towards a Theory of Transition*. New York: Monthly Review Press.

Mészáros, István 2010. *The Structural Crisis of Capital*. New York: Monthly Review Press

Antunes, Richard. 2010. Substance of Crisis, Introduction to Mészáros, István. 2010. *The Structural Crisis of Capital*. New York: Monthly Review Press

Scipes, Kim. 2010a. *AFL-CIO's Secret War against Developing Country Workers: Solidarity or Sabotage?*. Lanham, MD: Lexington Books

Scipes, Kim. 2010b. Why Labor Imperialism? AFL-CIO's Foreign Policy Leaders and the Developing World. *Working USA: The Journal of Labor and Society*. Vol 13, No 4. 465–479.

Task Force on Social and Solidarity Economy (TFSSE). 2014. Social and Solidarity Economy and the Challenge of Sustainable Development: Executive Summary of a TFSSE Position Paper. UNRISD; Available from: http://www.unrisd.org/ssetaskforce-positionpaper

CHAPTER 2

India's 'Informal Sector': Demystifying a Problematic Concept

In both academic and activist discourse, especially concerning India, the idea of the informal sector has come to prominence, particularly after India's liberalisation. This chapter demystifies the idea of the informal economy in India, revealing the multilayered existence of various groups of workers in vulnerable positions which are by no means inevitable or permanent but instead are the product of India's history and political economy. Accordingly, specific interventions have the potential to transform the lives of India's unorganised workers, but such policy would need to target the specialised requirements of each unorganised group of workers. We argue that the concept and discourse of the informal sectors imply the permanence of unorganised, unregulated work. Conceptualising Indian labour in this way leads to a position that the state should provide support and welfare measures to help workers survive at a bare minimum level of subsistence, but also to a fundamental failure to address the structural and specific causes of workers' vulnerabilities.

Therefore, any consideration of the possibility of going beyond capital, of impacting positive change on workers lives must necessarily start with a critique of the discourse of the informal sector. If, as is implied, the informal sector is a permanent new feature of the economy in India and elsewhere,

---

This chapter is an extended version of article titled 'India's "Informal Sector": Demystifying a Problematic Concept' authored by Timothy Kerswell and Surendra Pratap published in *Journal of Labor and Society*, John Wiley and Sons

T. Kerswell, S. Pratap, *Worker Cooperatives in India*,
https://doi.org/10.1007/978-981-13-0384-5_2

it becomes hard to imagine progress for the working class. The very concept of the informal sector serves the purpose of delegitimising alternatives to capital and capitalism. Thus, about any form of collective way of living and working, the idea of a permanent informal sector militates against the idea of social transformation. It is to this concept we now turn.

The working class in India had experienced a dramatic transformation of industrial relations after the liberalisation of the domestic economy and the expansion of the neoliberal capitalist economic agenda globally beginning in the 1980s. One of the defining aspects of this transformation is the process of *informalisation* of industries and workers. This chapter explains the historical origin and ongoing development of this process. The first section of the chapter summarises the current dynamics of the informal sectors in India. It then discusses how the process of *informalisation* has come to prominence from a historical perspective. The subsequent section puts forth some challenges in countering the process of informalizing industrial sectors and unorganised workers for the Indian working class. We argue that the concept and discourse of the informal sectors only suggest the state should provide support and welfare measures to help workers survive at a bare minimum level of subsistence, but fundamentally fail to address the structural and specific causes of workers' vulnerabilities.

The terms *informal sector* and *unorganised sector* are used interchangeably in India, and the National Commission for Enterprises in Unorganized Sector (NCEUS) defines the concept as follows:

> The unorganized (Informal) sector consists of all unincorporated (not covered under the factories act and the social security legislations like Employees State Insurance Act and Provident Fund Act) private enterprises owned by individuals or households engaged in the sale and production of goods and services operated on a proprietary or partnership basis and with less than ten total workers...Unorganised (Informal) workers consist of those working in the unorganised (Informal sector) enterprises or households, excluding regular workers with social security benefits, and the workers in the formal sector without any employment/social security benefits provided by the employers. (NCEUS 2009, p. 3)

This understanding of the informal sector and informal workers is also consistent with that of the International Labour Organization (ILO) and Women in Informal Employment: Globalizing and Organizing (WIEGO) (Chen and Vanek 2013, pp. 391–392).

In India, the informal sector constituted about 84 percent of the economy and the informal workers comprised about 92.3 percent of the total workforce in the mid-2000s (NCEUS 2007). However, on their own, these data are neither useful for understanding the reality nor for devising any significant policy initiatives to transform the reality. Agricultural workers in India, for example, constituted 64 percent of the informal sector workforce (NCEUS 2007), and the crisis in the agriculture sector, jobless growth and informalisation of the labour force in formal industrial sectors, directly or indirectly affected the dynamics of informalised work as a whole.

In the informal sector, 56 percent were self-employed, and only 36 percent were wage workers. In agriculture, as much as 64.2 per cent of workers were self-employed, while the rest were casual wage workers. In the non-agriculture informal sector, the self-employed constituted about 63 percent of the workforce, and only 37 percent were wage workers (17 percent regular wage workers and 20 percent casual wage workers). While wage employment dominated the formal sector (non-agriculture), the sector was also highly informalised, and contract and casual workers constituted a conservative estimate of 31 percent of the workforce (NCEUS 2007; Pratap 2015d). The percentage of non-agricultural workers in the informal sector rose from 32% to 36% between 1999–2000 and 2004–05, and the share of informal sector workers in the non-agriculture sector increased from 68 percent to 72 percent during this period (NCEUS 2007, 2009).

Increasingly, workers in the informal sector began integrating into the lowest levels of the global value chains. Product outsourcing from large to small firms grew, as did further subcontracting from the smaller companies to home workers. Almost 50 percent of the female self-employed manufacturing workers were home-based workers. National Sample Survey Organization surveys of informal manufacturing enterprises indicate that the incidence of subcontracting increased from 31 to 32 percent from 2000–01 to 2005–06. In some states, subcontracting was even more common; for example, it was 54 percent in West Bengal, 52 percent in Tamil Nadu, 39 percent in Karnataka and 35 percent in Uttar Pradesh (NCEUS 2007; Pratap 2015d).

The number of medium and small-scale enterprises (MSMEs) grew at 3.76 percent annually in the manufacturing sector and 0.47 percent for in the service industry between 2001–02 and 2006–07. The employment in these enterprises increased at an annual growth rate of 9.84 percent in the manufacturing sector and 2.06 percent in the service industry during the same period. This increase was closely linked to the expansion of global value chains and the integration of MSMEs in the value chains.

From 1999–00 to 2004–05, the number of workers in the economy increased from 396 million to 456 million, and most of this increase was in the informal sector. In the formal sector, the total increase in employment was only 7.7 million. In the formal non-agriculture sector, about 53.2 percent of the wage workers had no formal contract, and about 79 percent of the workers engaged in consistent, regular work were denied formal contracts (NCEUS 2007, 2009; Pratap 2015d). The above trends continued in 2005, and they reflect the dynamics of the informalisation by way of shifting jobs from the formal to the informal sector as well as the growing informalisation within the formal sector.

Indeed, the development dynamics emerged as jobless growth. In 1972 to 1983, the GDP grew at about 4.7 percent per annum accompanied by an employment growth rate of 2.44 percent. Then in 1983 to 1994, the GDP growth rate was about 5 percent, and job growth occurred at about 2.02 percent. In 1993 to 2005, the GDP growth rate reached 6.3 percent, but the job growth rate declined to 1.84 percent; and in 2004–05, the GDP growth rate rocketed to 9 percent, while the job growth rate was virtually stagnant at almost zero percent. Conversely, the increase in the labour force was consistently at over 2 percent (Papola and Sahu 2012; Pratap 2015d).

This reflects the multitude of people who annually enter the labour market and unable to find decent employment, survive in the informal sector as a reserve army of labour. Also, the new development dynamics are leading to the destruction of the livelihoods of many agricultural and forestry workers due to large-scale land acquisitions for industrialisation and urbanisation (see Kalshian 2007), and fish workers due to large-scale industrial fishing (Lahri 1998).

In 2004–05, about 77 percent of the population were living on less than Rs 20 per day, and 79 percent of the informal sector workers belonged to this poor and vulnerable group. Whereas 66.7 percent of regular wage workers belonged to this poor and vulnerable group, the remaining 33.3 percent were in the high-income group (Rs 93). Also, 74.7 percent of self-employed people fell into the poor and vulnerable group. Marginal farmers, fish workers, forestry workers, street vendors, scrap collectors and home-based workers constituted the vast majority of this group (NCEUS 2007, 2009).

The above picture leads us to two conclusions. First, the informal sector did not emerge as the natural outcome of economic development but as 'the outcome of deliberate policies to use the opportunities of globalisation to change the rules of the game. Institutional changes and new technological opportunities went hand in hand to create and impose the new economic model. Global capital mobility, global sourcing and comparatively easy options for relocation meant that the "successes" of lowering labour costs in one country transferred the structural pressures of the world market onto others' (ACTRAV 2011). Moreover, this is 'a social scandal of our time' (Martin 2013, p. 154).

Second, the informal sector is very diverse; transforming an informal sector worker's life and work requires a diverse range of targeted interventions and putting all these workers into one category of 'informal sector workers' is often confusing and misleading (see, for example, Agarwala 2013, p. 32). The crises of self-employed producers, self-employed service workers, home-based piece rate workers, formal sector contract workers and informal sector casual workers are entirely different, and different kinds of policy initiatives are needed to resolve their crises. The diversity of informal sectors poses challenges to transform these areas and the lives of those workers.

Surplus labour in the Indian economy has historical roots in Britain's colonial deindustrialisation of Indian industry and the forced transformation of India into a commodity economy in a context of imperialist exploitation (Patnaik 2009). The resolution of this problem demanded a path of economic development based on comprehensive land reforms to promote peasant agriculture and the expansion of labour-intensive manufacturing based on internal demand. This would have broken the vicious cycle hindering overall growth by absorbing the surplus population from agriculture and creating a sufficient demand for industrial goods in the vast rural areas. However, the path of development which independent India followed was never directed towards this, with the Indian bourgeoisie reaching a compromise with the landlord class and preventing thorough land reform (Patnaik 1999). India's economic development began facing a systemic crisis as early as the 1970s. The internal causes of the crisis were left unidentified and unaddressed. Instead, under the pressure of the new offensive of global capital, the resolution of this crisis was sought in external factors; thus, the economy was liberalised and integrated into the new global political economy with a new international division of labour.

Domestically, liberalisation came with entirely new dynamics. The social and political forces working for the transformation of economy and society were weakened due to: (a) downfall of the international socialist and democratic movements and the emergence of a unipolar world, (b) downfall and divisions in the working class movements leading virtually to its disintegration, (c) co-option of a large section of people's movements by national and international capital (by helping and promoting them) and the building or forcing of consent to work as a 'responsible' opposition within the framework of the new global political economy, (d) consensus built or forced among almost all of India's parliamentary parties, from right to left, on anti-labour economic policies and therefore a large section of the working class movement that was associated with these parties was paralyzed; (e) new global political economy and new international division of labour transformed the state into a corporate agent, and (f) new system of production and distribution based on global value chains that led to divisions and the scattering of the working classes, drastically reducing their collective strength and collective bargaining power (Pratap 2014).

In the new international division of labour, unorganised labour emerged as an essential source of profit maximisation. Value chains of various industries were established where almost all labour-intensive production activities were shifted to third world countries typically locked in the low organic composition of capital and where the cost of production including wages was meagre. Further profit maximization would depend on two factors: (a) unorganized labour in the third world countries mainly acting as a reserve army of labour and consistently putting downward pressure on wages and reducing the collective bargaining power of labour, and (b) cost of production reduced drastically by integrating the increasing sections of unorganized labour in the global value chains.

In these situations, foreign investment moved to those third world countries with greater reserve armies of labour, provided that the costs of other factors be more or less equal, including the infrastructure costs of production and the infrastructure costs of distribution. These factors related to the existence of competent subcontracting industries, the liberalisation of the economy and regional integration of economies and the existence of large national and regional markets. In these situations, with an imposed model of export-oriented growth, the third world countries, to attract sufficient foreign direct investment (FDI) and get sufficient export orders, are compelled to compete to offer better prospects of profit maximisation. The 'winners' in this competition are those countries who reduce the share of wages to the minimum by 'disciplining' labour and ensuring a significant supply of unprotected labour.

It is no coincidence that the ILO 'discovered' the dynamics of the so-called informal sector (ILO 1972, pp. 5–6) and started promoting an entirely new strategy for it, based on its division from the formal sector (ILO 1991, 2007, 2015), in the same period when the new international division of labour was taking shape. The vulnerabilities of organised labour were because these workers were not protected or organised into trade unions, and therefore the approach was aimed at organising and extending appropriate protections to them. This was also reflected in the report of the first National Commission on Labour (Government of India [GOI] 1969) that defined unorganized labour as those 'who have not been able to organize in pursuit of a common objective because of constraints such as (a) casual nature of employment, (b) ignorance and illiteracy, (c) small size of establishments with low capital investment per person employed, (d) scattered nature of establishments and (e) superior strength of the employer operating singly or in combination'. To transform the conditions of unorganized labour, the Commission recommended (a) periodically administering detailed surveys of unorganized labour to understand conditions, (b) legislative protection of unprotected/unorganized labour, (c) simplifying legislation and administrative procedures for small industries, (d) expediting education and organization of unorganized labour, (e) reinforcing and strengthening the inspection system to ensure labour rights, (f) protecting workers against middlemen, and (g) developing cooperatives and ensuring that the cooperatives pay adequate wages and bonuses to workers (Pratap 2014).

However, things are bit different in India. As the distinction between formal and informal sectors became officially institutionalised, the discourse of, and policy responses toward, the informal sector experienced a significant shift. In India, the term unorganised sector entered into systematic use in 1987 regarding reference of *The National Commission on Self-Employed Women*, set up under the chairpersonship of Ela Bhatt, the founder of the Self Employed Women's Association which will be discussed in Chap. 5. The first systematic attempt to define the informal sector was made in a workshop jointly organised by the National Council for Applied Economic Research (NCAER) and Self-Employed Women's Association-SEWA in 1997 (GOI 2002). When we use the term informal sector or unorganised sector, this conveys that these are no more transitional economies and that they cannot or need not be transformed, and the maximum we can do for informal sector workers is assisted survival at a bare minimum level of subsistence. Thus, the focus decisively shifts from transforming small economies and conditions of the unprotected labour force to maintaining them at this minimum level. It was consciously and purposefully accepted, and we were made to agree that unprotected labour and small economies may remain forever. It is in this background that the whole discourse on the issues of unorganised labour and small economies changed and took a new turn in the phase of liberalisation.

In what follows, we have a closer look at some notable legal and institutional changes in the politico-economic dynamics impacting the issue of unorganised labour (Pratap 2015a, b, c):

Before India's liberalisation, the public sector dominated the economy. The 18 most important industries were in the public sector and entirely controlled by the government. Moreover, 807 products of various kinds were reserved for the small-scale and tiny sectors. Social inclusion policies were inbuilt for public sector workers and small economies by way of reservations to socially excluded sections in providing employment and developing entrepreneurship. Highly subsidised inputs were provided to small economies and subsistence economies, as well as some secure markets, for their products.

Before liberalisation, India's labour movement was successful in forcing the government to regulate working conditions and extend social security and job security to large sections of workers.

Some legislation was passed to protect workers' employment from enterprise closure. The amendment of the Industrial Disputes Act in 1972 introduced a new clause making it compulsory for employers to give six months' notice to the government before closing an enterprise engaging 50 or more workers.

There were ground-breaking law changes achieved by the labour movement that led to the regularisation of hundreds of thousands of workers across sectors, which increased the power of the unions. The Contract Labour (Abolition and Regulation) Act was legislated in 1970 to prohibit the use of contract/casual labour in perennial activities of enterprises engaging 20 or more workers and to regularise casual workers involved in perennial activities.

The trade union movement was able to achieve some degree of regulation of working conditions ensuring some welfare benefits to workers who had been denied coverage under the Factories Act. For example, the Bonded Labour Abolition Act, 1976; Interstate Migrant Workmen's Act,

1979; the Workmen's Compensation Act Amendment in 1976 to remove the wage ceiling for its applicability; the Bidi and Cigar Workers (Conditions of Employment) Act, 1966; Equal Remuneration Act, 1976; Limestone and Dolomite Mines Labour Welfare Fund Act, 1972; Iron Ore, Manganese Ore and Chrome Ore Mines Labour Welfare Fund Act, 1976; Shops and Establishments Act.

The agriculture labour movement in India was appealing for central legislation for agricultural labour. The movement was victorious in Kerala and Tripura, where legislation was enacted (The Kerala Agricultural Workers Act, 1974 and The *Tripura Agricultural Workers Act,* 1986) that implemented a mechanism of tripartite conciliation and settlements and ensured some degree of social security and better collective bargaining power to agriculture labourers in these states.

The agrarian movements sought land reforms targeted at increasing the average size of land holdings and the distribution of land to landless workers by way of the equitable distribution of land. The successes and failures on this issue are very well reflected in the report of the Committee on State Agrarian Relations and Unfinished Task of Land Reforms published by the Ministry of Rural Development. Before liberalisation, effective initiatives emerged in various states for transforming the conditions of unorganised labour with an occupation-based approach.

Kerala was a pioneering state in designing and implementing legislation and policies to transform the conditions of unorganised labour setting up more than 20 welfare funds/boards. The boards are statutory bodies providing benefits such as medical care, education, and housing. Subsequently, an apex body was set up by the Kerala State Labour Authority Ordinance to coordinate, regulate, streamline, monitor and control the activities of the labour welfare schemes.

In Maharashtra, the Maharashtra Labour Welfare Board (MLWB), was constituted as a statutory body under the Bombay Labour Welfare and Fund Act, 1953 to promote the welfare of labourers and their dependents. All factories coming under the Factories Act, 1948 and all shops and establishments defined by the Bombay Shops and Establishments Act 1948 employing five or more persons, and all motor transport undertakings are coming under the Motor Transport Workers' Act, 1961, were covered under the act.

Tamil Nadu started with a state-level board and then initiated separate funds/boards for various occupations. The Tamil Nadu Manual Workers (Regulation of Employment and Conditions of Work) Act was enacted in

1982 and covered 55 occupations, including those traditionally informal ones, such as domestic workers and cycle repairs. Regulations and board were established to provide a broad range of social security benefits to workers. The board is tripartite and remains flexible to add more occupations and new schemes or benefits. Currently, it covers 60 occupations. The financing of the welfare board is based on contributions from employers, workers and the government.

To see the real dynamics of welfare boards, we may cite the example of The Kerala Fishermen Welfare Board and Maharashtra Mathadi, Hamal[1] and Other Manual Workers Welfare Board. The Kerala Fishermen Welfare Fund Board was established in 1986 under the Kerala Fishermen Welfare Fund Act, 1985. The board has three regional executives and 54 fisheries officers who look after 235 fishery villages. The board runs 15 schemes and provides a much more comprehensive range of benefits than those included in the ILO Convention on Minimum Standards of Social Security, for example, payment for fishing accident injury or assistance for funeral expenses. The tripartite dynamics of the board increase the collective bargaining power of the labour force. The Maharashtra Mathadi, Hamal and Other Manual Workers (Regulation of Employment and Welfare) Act was enacted in 1969 and created the Mathadi Tripartite Board. The Mathadi boards regulate the labour market by bringing all the workers into an organised setup, significantly increasing the collectivism and collective bargaining power of the workers. By and large, this strategy proved useful in extending protection to unorganised labour in the relevant sub-sectors. The enactment of the Building and Other Construction Workers (Regulation of Employment and Conditions of Service) Act, 1996 and Building & Other Construction Workers' Welfare Cess Act, 1996 were the last such initiatives using this approach (Pratap 2015b).

Working class movements in some areas sought to build collective dynamics by integrating small economies and deriving the benefits of economies of scale. There were some initiatives to form cooperatives of fish workers, forestry workers, agricultural workers, milk workers and mine workers. There were also some cooperative initiatives integral to the broader labour movement, which had a general impact on the working conditions in their occupational sector, and created a support base for the workers' movement in general, such as the cooperative initiatives of Chhattisgarh Mukti Morcha.

[1] Mathadi means loading-unloading workers and Hamal means head load workers.

These achievements of India's working class movement have been entirely reversed by the liberalisation of the Indian economy. In the new international division of labour, profit maximization of capital needs three kinds of workforce informalization: (a) informalization of the formal sector workforce; (b) shifting a significant proportion of production processes to the informal sector by integrating small units and home-based workers into global value chains; and (c) a huge reserve army of labour.

In this way, the unorganised labour or informal sector emerged as the source of profit maximisation in the new international division of labour. Therefore, the focus became maintaining the informal sector at the bare minimum level of subsistence, rather than enabling a transition from informality and vulnerability. Gradually, the formal sector was also informalized. From 1990, we observe almost no growth in protected/formal employment, for example, from 1999–00 to 2004–05, almost all incremental employment was informal, either in the form of informal sector employment or informal employment in the formal sector (NCEUS 2007, 2009). These trends continued in the later periods as well. Holdcroft (2013) notes that "the rapid increase in precarious work is being driven both by corporations and governments". The nature and character of state policy initiatives for labour in general and unorganised labour, in particular, reflect a focus on minimum standards for unorganised labour, rather than qualitative transformation of working and living conditions.

The picture of labour relations that emerge from the labour law amendments passed or in process at the central and state levels can be summarised as follows (Pratap 2015b, c):

Job security and comprehensive labour legislation will only apply to industries with 300 or more workers. In fact, very few industrial units come under this legal protection, because employers can get away by using apprentices or by an easy hire and fire system. No labour law will apply to household industries, and they will expand their linkages in the global value chain representing the space of the most exploited labour including child labour. The situation in small manufacturing units will likely be similar.

The right to strike is under severe attack. The requirement of 14 days' notice and conciliation proceedings means practically all industries are treated as protected public utility services where strikes or industrial action are legally tricky. It is not clear in the amendments whether workers in small factories will have the right to strike. The states are also taking similar initiatives to curtail the right to strike; for example, Andhra Pradesh and Tamil Nadu have already declared the automobile industry as a public utility service. Notably, the wave of strikes that emerged from 2005 mainly on the issue of freedom of association and collective bargaining and against the contract labour system has been the strongest in the automobile sector. Moreover the recent Gujarat Labour Laws (Gujarat Amendment) Bill 2015 prohibits striking in public utilities for two years (existing six months) and contains a new provision for settling various offences out of court.

Legislation changes have caused increasing health and safety problems. On the one hand, small factories (fewer than 40 workers) are excluded from the Factories Act. On the contrary, excessive overtime is gaining legal justification, and the list of hazardous industries and substances has been omitted from the new amendments.

Drastic changes in social security were initiated with a profound impact on the working class. In the name of extending social security to unorganised sector workers, the Unorganised Social Security Act 2008 was enacted to justify and institutionalise the duality and informalization of labour. With large-scale propaganda, some insurance schemes have been launched with the purpose of facilitating a process where corporations can further accumulate revenue from unorganised workers while silently scrapping workers' rights for free or affordable healthcare and compensation claims of industrial accidents. Moreover, FDI is now allowed in the insurance industry with access to the massive market in India. Pension laws, provident fund (PF) law and employees' state insurance are another issue area. Despite strong union opposition, the new pension scheme is being implemented in the railways and other government sectors, and also in the unorganised sector which shifts significant risk to workers and marketises insurance in India. The Employees' State Insurance (ESI) remained a lifeline for eligible industrial workers, yet it seems that the majority of workers will lose this lifeline as well. There have been attempts to privatise ESI hospitals, in line with the privatisation of the whole health sector. There have also been attempts to exclude most workers from ESI coverage. Most importantly, the government is now making the PF taxable.

The government is aggressively moving to amend the land acquisition law to facilitate the smoother acquisition of farmers' land for industrial and infrastructure projects. The law on food security is also going to be amended to reduce the coverage for the related population. The Land Reform Bill 2011 (Sinha 2011, Government of India 2013) was consciously and systematically ignored, and no one talks about it.

The landscape of industrial relations has changed dramatically after the economic liberalisation in India leading to questions about what the changes mean for India's working class and about the possibilities of transformation of the informal sector. First and foremost, we have to put the question of transforming the informal sector in the broader context of global capital-labour relations and the inherent drive toward capital accumulation under capitalism. Capital accumulation takes two forms: accumulation by appropriating the surplus value generated in the process of production and accumulation by means other than appropriating surplus value, such as primitive accumulation or accumulation by dispossession. Primitive accumulation reflects on the historical process that gave birth to the preconditions of a capitalist mode of production by way of unprecedented capital accumulation through land enclosures, usury, the slave trade, the looting of national assets by colonial powers, and by way of enforcing the separation of producers from the means of production. Primitive accumulation continues to be a significant form of capitalist expansion which persists until there are no resources or means of production left in the hands of the people in any part of the globe.

A puzzle is faced by the intellectual circles as to why in most third world countries was capital unable to separate a large population from the means of production, unable to absorb or destroy petty production and small economies in general, or why petty production or small economies continue to exist Kar (2012), Basu and Das (2008), Basole and Basu (2010), Patnaik (2006) and Foster-Carter (1978). One theoretical position is that the society has not yet developed to the capitalist stage and the democratic transformation of the society remains a major task. Advocates of this position are primarily in favour of independent, small economies. The alternate position argues that small economies are a significant hurdle to the building of collective/socialist consciousness and the socialist transformation of society; therefore, these intellectuals mainly welcome capital's current aggression against small production and small economies. In other words, one side stands with the workers but never goes beyond fighting mainly for the status quo, and the other side, implicitly regards primitive accumulation as a positive development, leading to proletarianization and an eventual anti-capitalist collective consciousness and the associated struggle for the socialist transformation of society. Both of these understandings appear to be the products of the same teleological understanding of the Marxist theory of capitalist development.

Capital indeed expands through expropriation or separation of producers from the means of production. This leads to the proletarianization of the whole society. The continued capitalist expansion in almost all third world countries indicates that this process exists everywhere. However, the pace and intensity of this process depend on the balance of power between labour and capital; the process of expropriating producers from the means of production is a class struggle, and in this class struggle, the producers cannot be considered a neutral or passive force. The nature and intensity of the class struggle and the balance of power between labour and capital depend on various factors. Moreover, in certain situations, it also may not appear to be a one-way process. The people, in their daily life struggles and broader political struggles, may be able to regain control over certain means of production and also recreate some means of production, subject to constant pressure from capital to expropriate them.

The expansion of capitalism in the third world started mainly after the end of colonialism. Colonial exploitation in these countries created enormous labour reserves that overburdened agriculture and compelled a significant population to survive on various precarious and low paid occupations. This created a vicious cycle hindering the growth of agriculture as well as secondary industry. Productive forces in overburdened agriculture remained arrested, and therefore the market for mass consumption goods also remained restricted, arresting industrial growth as well. Private capital was relatively weak, and this was the primary factor explaining why, in most of these countries, the state capitalist sector played a significant role in the capitalist development.

Under these conditions, and most importantly in the presence of the active working class movements that emerged as part of anti-colonial struggles, the balance of power was not decisively in favour of capital, and neither was the state in a position, nor was capital strong enough, to create a pace and intensity of expropriation and capitalist expansion comparable to industrial revolution Europe. The presence of strong land reform movements in most of these countries also explains the difference in dynamics as compared to European history. However, it does not mean that this process of primitive accumulation was absent.

If we look at the population expropriated/dispossessed from the means of production in India in just three decades after independence, while it may not be less than Europe, the pace and intensity may not be comparable to Europe. Moreover, this does not mean that small production remained outside capitalist exploitation. When capital takes control of the national economy through market expansion, it brings in control and integrates all the economies, in whatever form, under the capitalist system of exploitation. There are no small economies, for example in India, that are not integrated into the market. The nature of the crisis which small economies are currently facing was created by their integration into the capitalist economy, and they have been virtually converted to wage labour, even when they appeared to own the means of production and control the labour process.

It also appears to be an illusion created by a teleological understanding of social development that the new system is replacing the old one always takes its ideal form. Ideal 'modes of production' are only conceptual, and the actual forms tend not to possess all aspects of the ideal form. New modes of production always carry some aspects of the old, putting these in the service of the new, and transforming them. The same applies to the capitalist system. There can be no ideal capitalist system. The commonality is represented only by the dominance of the capitalist mode of production in the economy and its significant aspects that define the essential nature of the capitalist system.

A systemic crisis hit the Indian economy as early as the 1970s. The reasons for this crisis were internal, the primary factor being the absence of sweeping land reforms. The bourgeoisie's compromise with landlordism stifled productive forces in agriculture, kept the market for mass consumption goods restricted and slow to grow, progressively undermining the private capitalist sector. This led the ruling classes to enrich themselves from the public exchequer, representing a primitive accumulation of capital further limiting the growth of public investment (Patnaik 1999). At the same time, it is agreed that global capital entered into a systemic crisis in the 1970s, and the recoveries never returned to previous levels of growth (Foster 2008; Wallerstein 2009; Harvey 2010). With the OPEC-orchestrated oil crisis of 1973 and the global recession of 1980–82 created by record-high interest rates in the United States and Europe, resource prices collapsed throwing third world countries into a debt trap. The IMF–World Bank complex was then able to 'discipline' these countries with their structural adjustment programmes, and finally, the new global politico-economic regime of the WTO was born in 1995.

Under this new global politico-economic regime, national capitals were fully integrated into a global capital. International mobility of capital was institutionalised, and world production was restructured by the new international division of labour taking shape in global value chains. In these chains, the labour intensive operations were shifted to labour surplus third world countries, while the capital-intensive operations were kept under the strict control of imperialist countries. Through monopolistic control of finance, markets and branding, transnational corporations were able to capture the significant share of the revenue generated across the value chains. Moreover, the whole economy was increasingly informalised by informalising the workforce in larger industrial units and shifting labour-intensive production to smaller units and home-based workers.

During the same period, consent was reached among all the leading parliamentary parties on the policies of the new global politico-economic regime, creating a virtual vacuum for working-class politics. The result was a severe downturn in the working class movement, and the balance of power decisively shifted in favour of capital. This was also reflected in the rising share of profits and drastically declining share of wages. Therefore, the strategies that the global capital adopted to resolve its crisis, in turn, created a crisis for labour (Pratap 2014).

In this phase, we observe growth in the informal sector through an aggressive drive of capitalist expansion that emerged with the new global politico-economic regimes. This led to a large-scale, primitive accumulation of capital from natural resources, like land, water and forests, by large-scale land acquisition for industrialisation, infrastructure development and urbanisation projects, dispossession from livelihoods by the corporatisation of various sectors, like fisheries and waste management, and the liberalisation of retail. This also led to the most intensive exploitation of labour through workforce downsizing and replacement of high-wage formal workers with unprotected low-wage informal workers.

One significant impact of primitive accumulation is the growth of unemployment, drastically expanding the reserve army of labour and a crisis of survival for labour. This is one reason for the expansion of the informal sector as a survival strategy for workers in the reserve army of labour. Other sections of the growing informal sector are those increasingly integrated with global value chains, typically placed at the bottom of the value chains, for doing the most labour-intensive tasks in the most precarious conditions and with the least earnings such as small units, home-based workers and peasants engaged in contract farming.

In this background of changing global capital-labour relations, we can realise how the terminology, and indeed the concept of the informal sector itself, seems misleading and confusing, and even appears to be part of the design of the new global politico-economic regime. This is an important issue to reflect on when conceptualising the problems of the various sections of workers and consider strategies for transforming their working and living conditions.

The concept of the informal sector ignores the following aspects of unorganised labour in India:

> The persistence of small production and small economies in India resulting from three factors: weak national capital in the post-colonial period; workers' struggles to retain control of some means of production; pressure from a strong working-class movement on retaining small economies.

The growth and expansion of precarious petty economies and floating labour are not natural outcomes of development. They are consciously created by the policies of liberalization framed in accordance with the new international division of labour: (a) opening up previously protected sectors reserved for small economies to TNCs, privatization and monopolization by TNCs of industries providing inputs to traditional economies, and scrapping subsidies on inputs, created/increased vulnerability leading to the destruction of small economies; (b) large-scale accumulation by dispossession in large-scale land acquisition for industries leading to mass destruction of livelihoods both by destroying ecosystems and by corporatizing economies, such as allowing big companies in fishing; (c) the informalization of the economy was consciously done to maximize profits by intensifying labour exploitation through (i) scattering and expanding the value chains of industries and shifting a significant proportion of labour intensive operations to small economies and home-based workers who are consciously denied various labour rights, and (ii) by informalizing Labour in larger industrial units and converting protected labour to unprotected labour—that is, dispossessing them of their labour rights.

Including various sections of unorganised workers in a separate informal sector conveys two meanings: (a) their precarity and vulnerability are structurally permanent; at the most, their precarity and vulnerability can be reduced to some extent. (b) From this perspective, occupation-based policy initiatives for transforming life and work for various sections of workers becomes irrelevant, and the primary focus shifts to policy initiatives to enable survival at the bare minimum level of subsistence by extending some interest-free loans and some welfare like charity. Agarwala (2013, p. 58) has even argued that informal workers are encouraged by informal worker organisations to identify as informal workers as part of a new class identity, which seeks to obtain its political and economic goals through the state, rather than through class struggle. The initiatives of the state, and also those proposed by WIEGO and the ILO mostly remain restricted within this framework.

However, if we adopt the perspective of transforming life and work for various sections of unorganised labour, the vulnerabilities of the different sections of workers appear diverse and in need of different policy initiatives. Firstly, agriculture is the home of most (64%) informal sector workers (NCEUS 2007). The most significant problems of agricultural workers are as follows. (a) About 15 percent of them are landless, they depend on wage work, and there is no legislation governing their working conditions, except in the states of Kerala and Tripura. (b) Among farmers, 86 percent are marginal or small farmers (operating up to 2 hectares of land). They collectively account for only 45 percent of the total cultivated area, only 14 percent of the farmers are medium and large farmers operating more than 2 hectares of land, and they hold as high as 55 percent of the total cultivated area of the country (NCEUS 2007). (c) The forced dependency of farmers on markets. This involved the introduction of sterile or self-terminating seeds, imposing hybrid varieties that require vast amounts of fertilizer, pesticides and water, the monopolization of inputs by national and transnational corporations. Additionally there was the scrapping of subsidies on inputs by the state and the lack of focus on expanding infrastructure facilities for agriculture have increased the cost of inputs to the extent that cultivation in small fields is a business of loss, and the high level of fragmentation of land holdings has made the cultivation unsustainable. In these situations, agriculture emerges as a significant source of distress migration typically swelling the reserve army of labour which survives either as floating labour or by working in precarious occupations.

Therefore, an agrarian transformation would help to transform the lives and work of the informal sector workers, and this will be examined later in the case study of Menda village. However, the dominant discourse on the informal sector rarely focuses on agriculture. The importance of this sector is not seriously recognised where a negative driving factor could be transformed into a positive one. Instead, the discussions mainly focus on the poverty and suffering that stimulate justifications for providing farmers with assistance in the form of some welfare measures. The agrarian crisis can be resolved only through a series of sweeping reforms.

First, land reforms should be aimed at the equitable distribution of land holdings among farmers, accompanied by the promotion and institutionalisation of cooperative farming. Second, a sharp focus should be placed on building infrastructure for agriculture. Third, the state should end the corporate control of the lives of farmers by banning sterile seeds, researching new varieties which are better suited to the environment and require fewer market inputs. Fourth, there should be nationalisation or strict control of the trade of inputs and outputs related to agriculture. Agricultural subsidies have been provided across the world and cannot be abolished; however, the load of the subsidies can be reduced by relaxing the requirements of inputs from the market and by pursuing research and development to lower the cost of manufacturing the inputs. The self-employed producers in most of the traditional sectors of the economy are also facing some similar problems, and transforming their work and lives requires similar initiatives with occupation-specific dynamics.

Secondly, self-employed service workers face various specific challenges. However, fighting only to preserve the status quo may neither empower them to address these challenges nor offer improvement in their conditions. In their present situations, they may never be able to compete with the bigger players, and it may be only a matter of time before they are out of business. Empowering them and transforming the conditions of their lives and work demand the development of collective dynamics to reduce the cost of business and improve infrastructure along with increasing collective power.

Thirdly, in manufacturing, a significant proportion of small-scale units are also considered informal work for some larger industrial units in a buyer-driven value chain arrangement. Buyer companies engage with multiple suppliers to manufacture specific parts. By creating intense competition among suppliers, they consistently put downward pressure on them to reduce the prices of parts. There are also significant fluctuations in orders that buyers place with specific small-scale units; therefore, it is challenging for the small-scale units to engage workers on a regular basis (Kerswell and Pratap 2015, p. 544). The strategy within the small units is then to increase the vulnerability of labour and intensify labour exploitation to reduce the prices of parts, along with ensuring significant profits for themselves (Kerswell and Pratap 2015, p. 550). The state and the buyers overlook—and even justify—this injustice to which the workers are exposed in small enterprises. The whole game ultimately benefits the lead firms/brands whose supplier units and their employees are entirely engaged in doing the production work for the brands.

The brands used to undertake this production work themselves by engaging permanent workers, but now outsource the work to small suppliers. By so doing, they deny any responsibility towards the workers and suppliers, focusing solely on their profits. In general, they do not revise the prices of the parts manufactured by suppliers for years. The outsourcing system is one of the crucial features of the new production systems and also one of the new essential strategies of labour exploitation, by increasing the vulnerability and intensification of labour. However, there is currently no law regulating outsourcing.

In order to improve the working conditions in such small-scale enterprises, a new component of outsourcing practices must be added to the industrial relations law, with clear provisions for (a) brands or other first and second tier companies must prepare yearly contracts with supplier companies (rather than order-based contracts), and the cost of the total orders per year must include (apart from the expense of other factors and suppliers' profit margins) the total cost of wages, social security contributions, the cost of occupational health and safety, layoff wages and severance payment to workers if the orders are discontinued after a year (in case the supplier company is working for multiple brands and other customer companies, then the above total cost may be distributed among them accordingly); (b) the above cost breakup of the work orders showing the components of wages must be declared by the supplier company on its website, to ensure accountability, and in case of violations, the brands and suppliers can be made responsible and punished; and (c) the law must clearly state that the brands and other customer companies, whether national or foreign, are equally responsible for ensuring compliance with the labour standards across their value chain and for sharing its costs, and in case of any violations reported in their value chains, the brands may be made equally responsible and punished.

These initiatives may make it feasible to engage almost 90 percent of the workforce as regular workers in supplier companies, even if the work orders fluctuate drastically. This law may reduce the vulnerabilities of the supplier companies and their employees. Moreover, this will minimise the space for the suppliers' excuses for non-compliance with the labour standards and for engaging a large number of unreported workers and adversely affecting their lives. If this kind of legislation regarding outsourcing is enacted, it may also help improve the working conditions in such factory sectors, where the dynamics of outsourcing and informatization are creating hellish conditions for the workers, as in the whole garment industry.

Transforming the working conditions in small-scale industrial units, in general, may require significant policy changes to transform the dynamics of the trade relations in favour of small units. For example, some sectors and markets should be reserved for small economies; effective control should be placed on the rising input costs in the case of subsistence economies; and the trade relations between lead firms and the enterprises at the lower end of the value chain should be regulated. Formal long-term supply contracts should be made mandatory with clear criteria for determining and revising the prices of intermediary products in the case of industrial value chains. However, it is unlikely that the state will take such an initiative, without a strong working-class movement. Moreover, even if such policies are designed, in the absence of active workers' organisations, they may not induce any real change.

It is also vital that unions should manage relations between multiple actors and parties. In small-scale industries, structurally, the collective bargaining power of labour is minimal at the enterprise level. For any significant transformation of the working conditions to occur, they may also need to battle the exploitative relationship between brands and supplier companies, along with the struggles against their exploitation by the supplier companies. If the workers in the supplier companies can organise at the industry level, they may be able to compel the lead firms/brands to comply with their responsibility to establish long-term formal relations with enterprises and ensure the working conditions and labour standards across the value chains. Furthermore, this may constitute the basis of broader solidarity between the labour at the lower and higher levels of the value chain.

The real dynamics of industry-level organising and collective bargaining in small-scale industries has not yet strongly emerged in India. However, in recent decades, there have been some industry-wide strikes in various small-scale sectors. This indicates the direction of the working class movements in such sectors. For example, there was an industry-wide strike of more than 150 power looms in Ludhiana, Punjab in 2011 (Amritpal 2014), an industry-wide strike in 200 tea gardens in West Bengal in 2012 (ITUC 2012) and an industry-wide strike in 25 hot-rolling steel factories in Delhi in 2014 (Staff Reporter 2013). All these strikes were mostly demands for the implementation of minimum labour standards in the sector.

The issue of informalization of the workforce in larger industrial units or the formal sector and the inclusion of these workers in the informal sector most powerfully exposes the fact that the whole concept of the informal sector is part of the design of the new global politico-economic regime and is integral to the new profit-maximizing strategies under the new international division of labour. It institutionalizes and justifies informalization. The very concept has reversed the working class' victories on this issue, reflected in the enactment of the Contract Labour Abolition and Regulation Act that led to the regularisation of thousands of workers across sectors and the country. There is no logic or justification for the informal status of these workers; in fact, it is an open injustice against these workers.

The ILO and WIEGO initiatives propose the formalisation of these informal workers but never argue for the end of the informal/contract labour system in these industries. By contrast, the working class movements are actively demanding an end to the informal contract labour system, and in several recent struggles, they have also achieved some victories towards the regularisation of casual and contract workers. For example, in 2013–14, Honda Motorcycles and Scooters India Ltd. (HMSI) and Maruti Suzuki in Manesar, Haryana agreed on a policy for gradually regularising contract workers (Pratap 2015d). In 2010, a trade union struggle achieved the regularisation of 452 temporary workers in the Horlicks factory in Nabha, Punjab (Rossman 2013). Similar victories were reported[2] in some industrial units in Maharashtra, including the regularisation of 192 contract workers in the tractor plant of Mahindra and Mahindra in Pune in 2012–13, the regularisation of 45 contract workers in Jai Industries (Cement) in Nagpur.

One of the most notable achievements of the wave of strikes mainly from 2005 onwards is that the working class movements were successfully able to unite the permanent and contract workers and, to a great extent, were able to defeat the strategy of creating a divide between them in many factories. In most of these struggles, the issue of contract workers was raised prominently. The Maruti Suzuki struggle (continuing since 2011) carried this wave to its culmination when the demand to end the contract labour system was raised clearly and forcefully, and solidarity between permanent and contract workers reached the extent that the second occupation of the factory was reinstating contract workers dismissed during the struggle.

[2] This was reported by Mr. Amrut Meshram, CITU General Secretary Pune, in an interview conducted in November 2015, as part of a study on Conditions of Workers in Forestry and Wood Based Sector in Maharashtra conducted by one of the authors of this chapter for Building and Wood Workers International (BWI), South Asia Office, New Delhi. The report of the study is to be published soon.

Conclusion

The above accounts indicate that the nature of vulnerability and its causes differ in various sections of unorganised workers. Therefore, different policy initiatives and strategies on organising and collective bargaining are needed to empower the workers in diverse occupations to transform their working and living conditions. However, in reality, there is no great focus on identifying the specific vulnerabilities in various occupations or the causes of these vulnerabilities, and there is no focus on addressing the specific causes to end the vulnerabilities. Moreover, there is almost no focus on empowering workers to transform the reality themselves. Even the most positive state policy initiatives, with occupation-specific foci, have systematically avoided such provisions that genuinely empower workers, and in so doing, have degraded them to charity.

It is also evident that vulnerability is not permanent, and conditions may be transformed to help workers address the vulnerability. However, the concept of the informal sector is based on the presumption that vulnerability is permanent, and therefore it mostly articulates common vulnerabilities, such as low incomes and unsafe/unhealthy working conditions, suggesting means of support and welfare measures to help the workers survive at the bare minimum level of subsistence.

Last but not the least, the nature of the crisis and vulnerabilities that various unorganised workers are facing are linked with the liberalisation of the economy and the new international division of labour established under the new global politico-economic regime. It is incredibly difficult for individual workers to survive and face the challenges created by the new dynamics of the trade relations and labour relations. In the current situation, fighting to maintain the status quo may neither help workers improve working conditions nor empower them to meet such challenges. To transform the reality, a higher level of collectivism is needed and its form may be different in different occupations. The general nature of collectivism may be one that promotes a collective way of living and working and, by these dynamics, reduces the cost of living, empowers the workers to focus on their overall development and increases their collective bargaining power and political power in the society.

Trade unions and other mass organisations of workers form the base of collectivism, but do not automatically create collectivism. The dynamics of collective ways of living and working represent the most essential aspect of collectivism, and these can be achieved by creating collective institutions that promote collective modes of living and working. However, the attempts to build collectivism, such as cooperatives of workers, delinked to the working class movements and class organisations of workers, generally end up as business collectives rather than workers' collectives.

References

ACTRAV. 2011. *From precarious work to decent work. Policies and regulations to combat precarious employment.* ILO: Geneva. Available from: http://www.ilo.org/wcmsp5/groups/public/---ed_dialogue/---actrav/documents/meetingdocument/wcms_164286.pdf

Agarwala, Rina. 2013. *Informal Labor, Formal Politics and Dignified Discontent in India.* New York: Cambridge University Press.

Amritpal. 2014. A Report on Ludhiana textile workers strikes and the owners' propaganda. Available from: http://sanhati.com/articles/4246/

Basole, A and Basu, D. 2010. Relations of production and modes of surplus extraction in India. Working Paper no. 109, Economics Department, University of Massachusetts Amherst. Available from: http://scholarworks.umass.edu/cgi/viewcontent.cgi?article=1108&context=econ_workingpaper

Basu, D & Das, D. 2008. *Political economy of contemporary India: some comments on Partha Chatterjee's theoretical framework.* Available from: http://sanhati.com/excerpted/1045/#sthash.p13ZNUKk.dpuf

Bellamy Foster, J. 2008. The financialization of capital and the crisis. *Monthly Review*, Vol. 59, No. 11. p1

Chen, MA & Vanek, J. 2013. Informal employment revisited: theories, data & policies. *The Indian Journal of Industrial Relations.* Vol. 48, No. 3. pp390–401

Foster-Carter, A. 1978. The modes of production controversy. *New Left Review.* Vol. I, No. 107. pp47–78

Government of India. 1969. *The Report of National Commission on Labour.* Ministry of Labour and Employment and Rehabilitation, Available from: https://casi.sas.upenn.edu/sites/casi.sas.upenn.edu/files/iit/National%20Commission%20on%20Labour%20Report.pdf

Government of India. 2002. *The report of Second National Commission on Labour*, Ministry of Labour and Employment, Available from: http://www.prsindia.org/uploads/media/1237548159/NLCII-report.pdf

Government of India. 2013. *Draft National Land Reforms Policy 2013.* Department of Land Resources, Ministry of Rural Development, Available from: http://dolr.nic.in/dolr/downloads/pdfs/Draft_National_Land_Reforms_Policy_July_2013.pdf

Harvey, David. 2010. *The Enigma of Capital and the Crises of Capitalism*. London: Profile Books.

Holdcroft, J. 2013. Implications for union work of the trend towards precarization of work. *International Journal of Labour Research*. Vol. 5, No. 1. pp41–57

International Labour Organization. 1972. *Employment, Wages and Equity: A Strategy for Increasing Productive Employment in Kenya*. International Labour Office: Geneva.

International Labour Organization. 1991. *The dilemma of the informal sector.* Report of the Director General (Part I) to the International Labour Conference 78th Session, International Labour Office: Geneva.

International Labour Organization. 2007. *Background document, Tripartite Interregional Symposium on the Informal Economy: Enabling Transition to Formalization*. International Labour Office: Geneva.

International Labour Organization. 2015. *Transition from the Informal to Formal Economy Recommendation, 2015 (No. 204)*. 104th ILC session, 12 June 2015, Geneva, Available from: http://www.ilo.org/dyn/normlex/en/f?p=NORML EXPUB:12100:0::NO::P12100_ILO_CODE:R204

ITUC. 2012. *Annual survey of violations of trade union rights*. Available from: http://survey.ituc-csi.org/India.html?lang=en

Kalshian, R. 2007. *Caterpillar and the Mahua Flower: Tremors in India's Mining Fields*. Panos South Asia: New Delhi. Available from: www.panossouthasia.org

Kar, G. 2012. *The Semi-Feudal Character of Indian Agriculture*. Available from: http://sanhati.com/excerpted/8197/

Kerswell, T &Pratap, S. 2015. Informality in automobile value chains in India. *WorkingUSA: The Journal of Labor and Society*. Vol. 18, No. 4. pp533–553

Lahiri, S. 1998. Imperialist globalisation of the Indian seas and the fishworkers Struggles. *Revolutionary Democracy*. Vol. IV, No. 2. Available from: http://www.revolutionarydemocracy.org/rdv4n2/fishwork.htm

Marin, E. 2013. Precarious work: an international problem. *International Journal of Labour Research*. Vol.5, No.1. p153

National Commission for Enterprises in the Unorganized Sector. 2007. *The report on conditions of work and promotion of livelihoods in unorganized sector.* Government of India: New Delhi.

National Commission for Enterprises in the Unorganized Sector. 2009. *The challenge of employment in India, an informal economy perspective*. National Commission for Enterprises in the Unorganised Sector, Government of India: New Delhi.

Papola TS & Sahu, PP. 2012. *Growth and structure of employment in India: long-term and post-reform performance and the emerging challenge*. Institute for Studies in Industrial Development, New Delhi.

Patnaik, P. 1999. Capitalism in Asia at the end of the millennium. *Monthly Review.* July–August.

Patnaik, P. 2006. *The need to protect petty production*. Available from: http://www.macroscan.com/anl/jul06/pdf/Petty_Production.pdf

Patnaik, P. 2009. Socialism and the Peasantry. *Social Scientist*, Vol. 37, Iss 11/12.

Pratap, S. 2014. Emerging trends in factory Asia: international capital mobility, global value chains, and the labour movement. Asia Monitor Resource Centre: Hong Kong.

Pratap, S. 2015a. *The political economy of labour law reforms in India—part I*. Available from: http://sanhati.com/excerpted/13633/

Pratap, S. 2015b. *The political economy of labour law reforms in India—part II*. Available from: http://sanhati.com/excerpted/13633/

Pratap, S. 2015c. *The political economy of labour law reforms in India—part III*. Available from: http://sanhati.com/excerpted/13633/

Pratap, S. 2015d. The informality and precarious work in production chain capitalism: A case study of automobile industry in India. *Asian Labour Journal*. Vol 1

Rossman, P. 2013. Establishing rights in the disposable jobs regime. *International Journal of Labour Research*. Vol.5, no.1. p31

Sinha, Ashish. 2011. Jairam Ramesh keen to bring Land Reforms Bill in Parliament, *India Today*. Available from: http://indiatoday.intoday.in/story/jairam-ramesh-keen-to-bring-land-reforms-bill/1/150949.html

Staff Reporter. 2013. Wazirpur hot-rolling steel plant workers call off strike. *The Hindu*. Available from: http://www.thehindu.com/todays-paper/tp-national/tp-newdelhi/wazirpur-hotrolling-steel-plant-workers-call-off-strike/article4628854.ece

Wallerstein, I. 2009. *Crisis of the capitalist system: where do we go from here?* Available from: http://mrzine.monthlyreview.org/2009/wallerstein121109.html

CHAPTER 3

The Rise and Fall of the Chhattisgarh Mines Shramik Sangh and Its Cooperative Movement

In the Indian mining town of Dalli-Rajhara, a unique social experiment took place which constituted an important part of both trade union history and the cooperative movement in India and has broader relevance for the union movement globally. This chapter provides the rise and fall of the Chhattisgarh Mines Shramik Sangh (Chhattisgarh Mine Workers Movement) (CMSS henceforth), with a focus on the formation of the union, its significant achievements and its later decline.

The chapter argues that the union's decline was not an inevitable result of globalisation, but was the result of specific fundamental weaknesses in the leadership structure of the union, and some of its strategy and tactics. The chapter utilises the literature on resource mobilisation theory to frame this argument, and the CMSS case strengthens this perspective, particularly against alternative paradigms which attempt to explain the rise and fall of social movements.

CMSS built a powerful cooperative movement with an influence well beyond industrial unionism. The movement's concept was revolutionary in India and marked the first time a trade union went beyond industrial concerns. CMSS advocated for 24/7 unionism, the idea that the union should be an essential part of the workers' lives always, as a model for unions in general, but particularly when organising contract labourers.

Despite these achievements, the union faced critical problems. Some inbuilt weaknesses in its work contributed to an inability to respond to these problems and its eventual decline. The history of CMSS demonstrates

T. Kerswell, S. Pratap, *Worker Cooperatives in India*,
https://doi.org/10.1007/978-981-13-0384-5_3

the importance of choosing the right strategy to respond to changing political and economic circumstances as a vital part of building an effective social movement union. This chapter will demonstrate that, among its other problems, CMSS did not respond adequately to India's liberalisation. Nonetheless, the history of CMSS is a case study in the possibilities that cooperative formation presents, but also the contradictions that can emerge from a new and innovative type of unionism.

CMSS was the first union in India to orient its struggles towards issues faced by precariously employed contract workers, in this case, those who worked in the mines. Before the efforts of CMSS, unions in Dalli-Rajhara, including even the Communist Party of India's unions, only organised formal sector workers who were permanent employees of the government-owned mines' operator, the Bhilai Steel Plant (BSP).

The Bhilai Steel Plant was founded in Bhilai, Chhattisgarh with the assistance of the Soviet Union in 1959. Before its construction, "Bhilai was a small village in Durg district, in the Chhattisgarh region of Madhya Pradesh, central India" (Parry 2008, p. 233). On the one hand, the BSP was significant in developing India's economic self-reliance (Menon and Nigam 2007, p. 166), and in generating national employment. On the other hand, the impact on the local region was also significant as the construction of the plant and its associated dams displaced large numbers of Adivasi[1] villagers.

Parry (2003, p. 217) has extensively documented that most employees of the Bhilai Steel Plant were from 'all over India'. Despite the impact of displacement on the Adivasi population, the high-quality employment, and the associated benefits, generated by the BSP had little impact on the Adivasi population. Adivasis tended to end up in the contract labour system, particularly in the mining town of Dalli-Rajhara whose abundant supply of iron ore serviced the Bhilai Steel Plant. Dalli-Rajhara is a remote town which exists between the two primary mines of the region, namely Dalli and Rajhara Mines. The town is a single industry town, with the mines being the predominant employer. The rest of the town is made up of trading communities which service the miners.

[1] Literature in Indian political science interchangeably refers to villagers who live/d according to traditional ways of life with geographical isolation, 'backward' [sic], distinctive culture, language and religion and 'shyness of contact' [sic] (Government of India, Labour Bureau 2007, p. 6) as Adivasis, 'Tribals', Tribal People's or Indigenous peoples as opposed to those Indians who have been fully integrated into the capitalist labour market and the so-called 'mainstream' of Indian society.

The contract workers in Dalli-Rajhara performed brutal mining tasks such as razing mine sites, crushing ore into smaller pieces and then 'head loading[2]' the ore into trucks. This group of workers formed the initial base of CMSS membership. At its height, CMSS commanded a membership base of approximately 10,000 workers per Ganesh Chaudhari, the current general secretary of CMSS (Personal communication, 22 June 2015). The events in this chapter describe the genesis of CMSS which took place in the mid-1970s and trace its growth as a movement in the 1980s, and eventual decline coinciding with the assassination of leader Shankar Guha Niyogi and the beginning of India's liberalisation in 1991. This chapter explains the factors which led to the movement's rise and fall.

The basic chronology of the CMSS movement is as follows. The movement can be said to begin after the widespread defection of contract workers from rival unions to CMSS in 1977. This event gave CMSS control over the contract mining workforce, as well as the cooperative societies themselves which were previously run by the rival unions. In 1979, the Union won a decisive battle in preventing the full mechanisation of the Dalli-Rajhara Mines, successfully proposing the semi-mechanization of the mines which allowed retention of most of the workforce in exchange for higher levels of productivity.

The struggle for the rest of the 1980s would centre on the question of productivity and mechanisation levels of the mines, and the strategic use of Voluntary Retirement Schemes by the Bhilai Steel Plant to deplete the unionised workforce. The union responded to its increasingly fragile position by attempting to organise in neighbouring industries and regions in Chhattisgarh. In response to this, in 1991, the movement's leader, Niyogi, was assassinated in Bhilai, Chhattisgarh and shortly after this the movement fractured according to various personal and political disagreements. In 1994 the management of the Bhilai Steel Plant agreed to the absorption of any remaining cooperative society workers who had begun their employment before 1975 in a process that eventually ended in 1996. After 1996, the cooperative societies dissolved, and CMSS cooperative movement came to an end. While the movement remains today, it has a fraction of the influence it had at its high point, and rival unions have taken its place.

[2] Literally carrying the ore in a vessel balanced on top of their heads from the crushing site to the truck.

The Resource Mobilization framework initially developed by McCarthy and Zald (1977) significantly improved social movement research. This perspective argued against 'grievance' perspectives or theories that suggested that the primary driver in the level of social movement activity were the number of grievances in the overall society (McCarthy and Zald 2002, p. 533). McCarthy and Zald noted a concomitant rise in affluence in American society and a corresponding increase in the number of social movements, which led them to an economistic theory suggesting a causal link between social movements and the economic resources which activists could mobilise (Ibid). McCarthy and Zald concluded that necessary components of rising social movements were "expanded personal resources, professionalisation, and external financial support available to movements in advanced industrial societies… [along with] professional movement organisations" (McAdam et al. 1996, p. 3).

McCarthy and Zald's theory was criticised for its narrow economistic conclusions, to the extent that even the authors accept some level of criticism of their theory (Ibid; Zald 2000, p. 2). Critics point to the inevitable conclusion that groups with limited economic resources are perceived incapable of effecting social change and that this perspective marginalises the role of grievances, culture and identity amongst other factors in its analysis (Kendall 2005, p. 531). Against this, it is possible to contrast the more political approaches to Resource Mobilization theory advocated by Tilly and McAdam as well as the new social movement theories which emphasised: "movement decentralisation, informal participation and grassroots democracy" (Fantastia 1988; Rosenthal and Schwartz 1989).

Tilly (1977, Chapter 1, p. 11) for example proposes a 5-part framework to explain the success or otherwise of collective action including shared interests, the structure of an organisation, the mobilisation of resources (both economic and non-economic), the opportunity to exert power, and the practice of collective action itself. This framework goes a long way toward helping to answer the fundamental research question for this chapter. It contributes to an explanation of the meteoric rise of an organisation as unique as CMSS within the context of Indian labour politics, where unions appear to be dependent on patronage from political parties or substantial amounts of funding from international sources. Additionally, what explains the decline of the movement and its marginalisation from the political scene?

In explaining the rise and fall of CMSS, this chapter will argue that the movement was successful when it mobilised specific political resources.

The union had a highly disciplined organisation, led by a close-knit, vanguardist leadership, and cemented by a charismatic leader in the form of Shankar Guha Niyogi whose own legitimacy and political positions emerged out of his participation in a great era of debate in Indian labour politics. CMSS also possessed a unique legitimacy as the representative of the contract workers which it leveraged to gain control over and then extend a movement of cooperative societies, and in turn, create new public goods such as Shaheed Hospital and the peasant movement. In turn, it fell as it lost its political resources because of weakness in its organisational structure which upon Niyogi's assassination created the ground for the splintering of the movement, and its economic resources due to its inability to retain a place for semi-mechanized mining in Dalli-Rajhara.

Both the erosion of financial resources through a loss of control of the mines and political resources regarding workforce attrition and the splintering of the movement, constitute a better explanation for the fall of CMSS than the alternative hypotheses which from grievance theory or new social movement theory. Notably, the grievances of contract workers are enduring and if anything, even exacerbated in comparison to the high point of CMSS' activism, which rules out grievance theory as an explanation. Further to this, the identity and culture of the workers in question have remained stable throughout the existence of CMSS as has the political actors' framing of political struggles. We thus reject new social movement theory as an explanation of the movement's fall.

An unfortunate feature of much scholarship in the 'cultural turn' or the result of post-modernist influence in the social sciences is an overemphasis on identity concerns in explaining political formations, including social movements. These findings regarding CMSS help demonstrate the enduring relevance of the more political versions of Resource Mobilisation Theory. This includes what Zald (2000, p. 1) considers "ideologically structured action" or "behaviour which is guided and shaped by ideological concerns-belief systems defending and attacking current social relations and the social system" (Ibid, p. 3).

Identity concerns just did not register as a significant factor in our interviews with mine workers and union activists, irrespective of their economic status or position on the political spectrum. Thus, the movement's class focused nature, which would no doubt be considered 'old left' by aspects of contemporary social movement scholarship, cannot be taken seriously as an explanation for the movement's fall. The workers identified themselves only as 'mazdoors' (labourers), and indeed, the workers who have dropped out of the orbit of CMSS have been picked up by alternative class-based organisations as will be discussed below.

CMSS built a powerful cooperative movement with an influence well beyond industrial unionism. The union set up a hospital, promoted collective farming and peasant activism in the countryside, defended slum occupants in the towns and cities and competed in elections. CMSS advocated for '24/7 unionism', the idea that the union should be an important part of the workers' lives always, as a model for unions in general, but particularly when organising contract labourers.

Despite these achievements, the Union faced two fundamental tensions which undermined its power leading to its decline. The first was a political struggle which occurred after the assassination of the movement's leader, Shankar Guha Niyogi, in 1991. The highly centralised nature of CMSS was a fundamental weakness. Niyogi was the sole strategic thinker and ideologue of the movement. His failure to groom a successor meant his assassination was a severe blow. Following his assassination, second-tier leaders would vie for power, splintering the movement and weakening its legitimacy.

Secondly, the union was unable to establish control over the terrain of struggle due to its ideological limitations. The strategy of the union invested resources into the goal of 'departmentalisation' under the auspices of the Bhilai Steel Plant. Departmentalisation represented a kind of mid-way point between the status of a contract worker and that of a regular worker that involved gaining security of employment but without some of the other benefits such as retirement pensions. The theory of the union was to establish more permanence in the workforce to strengthen the bargaining position of the workers in the union.

Instead, the union lost power, as the Indian government used a combination of the natural attrition of departmentalised unionists, voluntary redundancy schemes and the mechanisation of the mining process to marginalise union influence in Dalli-Rajhara. Governmental pressures associated with India's liberalisation in the early 1990s exacerbated this process. Accordingly, CMSS lost strength, and the Indian government re-established contract labour in Dalli-Rajhara without the cooperative movement standing in its way.

Moody (2002, p. 58) has argued that '[t]he vision appropriate to the era of globalisation is social-movement unionism'. In conceptualising social movement unionism, Seidman (1994, p. 2) notes that "Theoretically, social movement unionism is perhaps best defined as an effort to raise the living standards of the working class as a whole, rather than to protect individually defined interests of union members". CMSS indeed represented a social movement union, long before there was a theory to conceptualise it as such. The CMSS example demonstrates that while social movement unionism is more effective than other forms, it still faces specific challenges because of neoliberal globalisation. The history of CMSS shows the importance of choosing the right strategy to respond to changing political and economic circumstances as a vital part of building an active social movement union.

Hensman (2011), has argued workers' strategies must reflect what she sees as the realities of globalisation with India providing successful (or otherwise) examples of this. Both Hensman and Agarwala (2013, p. 16) have argued that the so-called informal sector is necessarily a permanent part of the economic structure of India and even an integral part of workers' identities, which they supposedly leverage as a voting bloc to extract gains from the state. The entrenchment of the informal sector leads Agarwala to argue workers should make citizenship-based claims against the state rather than union claims against employers. The example of CMSS demonstrates that organising efforts can be successful in a mostly informal, and increasingly globalised, economy. Instead, poor strategic and tactical choices explain the decline of CMSS rather than the usual post-globalisation narrative of the decline of trade unions. The progressive weakening of the unions' position has several causes. Its political strength and unity have weakened. Because of this, the mechanisation and unionisation of the mines have diverted the union from its 24/7 union model toward a servicing union model, defensively maintaining the position of its dwindling membership. No longer does the union fight its battles in the streets; it has been successfully pacified and reduced to the courts.

The chapter begins by outlining the methodology of the study, before describing the historical, political and economic context of the CMSS movement's genesis. Here CMSS is positioned within the broader spectrum of Indian labour politics, and provide some understanding as to how CMSS developed their innovative political views. While the capacity to innovate is one of the critical resources the union had, the overreliance on Niyogi as a charismatic leader, the over-centralization of power around him, and the inability to generate a new generation of leaders is a significant weakness.

Following this, there is a discussion of key events in the founding of the CMSS movement, allowing us to highlight the strategies and tactics of the movement and some of the union's vital resources. These included its legitimacy as the representative of contract workers and the demand for contract workers to transition into permanent work status. Our analysis sits in contrast with perspectives which suggest the permanence and even desirability of informality in India as a fundamental assumption of labour organising (Agarwala 2013). On the other hand, the movement lost critical resources as it was unable to adequately respond to the strategy and tactics of the Bhilai Steel Plant management, which led it to lose control over the economic terrain of Dalli-Rajhara and depleted the presence of the unions and the cooperatives in the mines.

Finally, the role of CMSS in the cooperative movement is discussed, highlighting the way that CMSS was able to gain control of the movement. Following this, there is a discussion of the ways that CMSS revolutionised the cooperatives as instruments of workers power, utilising them to extend the influence of the union and make critical interventions for the working class in Dalli-Rajhara.

Methodology

This chapter is the result of a lengthy investigation in Dalli-Rajhara undertaken in the summer of 2015 as part of a larger research project in India studying trade union-led cooperatives. The research aimed to use a combination of ethnographic methods and oral history to document the CMM movement and its efforts to build collective ways of living and working and to understand the movement's rise and later decline. During this time, the movement was observed and investigated by the researchers. We utilized judgement sampling and felt that the key leaders of the movement would likely provide the most valuable information and thus prioritized obtaining their data first. Top leaders were also able to source additional interview subjects via snowball sampling.

The researchers were thus able to interview the movement's top leaders, leading union activists and many of the rank and file workers who were members of CMSS, as well as leading political figures and rural peasant activists from their political arm, Chhattisgarh Mukti Morcha (CMM). The researchers also interviewed farmers, doctors, teachers and cultural activists associated with the movement in Dalli-Rajahara, Dondi Lohara and Raipur, Chhattisgarh.

This investigation was corroborated by interviews with rival unions in Dalli-Rajhara such as the Communist Party of India–run All India Trade Union Congress (AITUC) and the Communist Party of India (Marxist)–run Centre for Indian Trade Unions (CITU), both significant unions in Dalli-Rajhara. While CMSS did not publish large amounts of material, we recovered some primary documents from the union. We further corroborate the data through secondary sources which have studied the movement with a different focus in mind.

The lack of a recorded history of the CMSS movement means there are few if any, alternatives to the data collection methods used. Despite this, it is important to note the advantages and disadvantages of the methods of this study. The main benefit of this interviewing strategy was that it obtained first-hand accounts of the movement by those who had actively participated in it, including many long-time activists who were present at the genesis of the movement and were close comrades of its leader, Shankar Guha Niyogi.

There are, however, limitations regarding this approach which had practical relevance regarding the data collection efforts. It was difficult for many of the long-time activists to come to terms with the declining influence of the union causing a degree of romanticising in their responses. We broke this down through persistent questioning and corroboration of data from multiple (including rival political) sources. In one such example, a group of contract workers believed they had 'won' the right to guaranteed employment until a retirement age, but the union would not produce any documentation as evidence of this. An interview with a rival union produced a primary source document, signed by the various unions of the region including CMSS that there would be a retirement age, but without any such guarantee of employment. The example demonstrates the critical role of political influence in generating misconceptions among interview subjects. These factors were mitigated through extensive interviewing across multiple rival sources.

Similarly, it was necessary to take into account the role of memory in the data collection process, especially since some of the events considered in this study occurred almost 40 years from the time of the interview. We mitigated this by conducting multiple rounds of interviews with subjects on any issues which were revealed as being contentious from an empirical standpoint.

Historical, Political and Economic Context of the Rise of CMSS

Historical Context

CMSS emerged in the 1970s with India in crisis. There were fiscal problems associated with the war with Pakistan in 1965, the oil shock of 1973 and a food crisis. Working class and national self-determination movements became radicalised creating a severe challenge for the state.

The economic crisis was such that it demanded a decisive shift in economic policies, either to the left or the right. Imperialist pressure to liberalise the economy increased, reflected in conditions imposed by the U.S. and the International Bank for Reconstruction and Development. Additionally, there was pressure from right-wing political forces both within and outside of the governing Congress party.

Despite this, India was not yet ready to risk its economic and political independence. Rather than succumbing to imperialist pressure, then-Prime Minister Indira Gandhi adopted radical nationalist and welfarist policies. The policies attempted to pacify movements of national self-determination, and some pro-labour policies were adopted to promote industrial peace (Chaudhury 1977). The goal of Gandhi's political platform was growth and stability with a goal of self-reliance (Malik 1988), with a particular emphasis on developing food security, expansion of agriculture infrastructure, domestic input production and limited land reforms.

The government shifted economic and social policies to the left albeit within the confines of radical nationalism. However, large-scale repression was unleashed in response to the upsurge of working class and national self-determination movements and the strong right-wing opposition both within and outside the Congress Party, culminating in an emergency suspension of democracy from 1975 to 1977 (Palmer 1976, p. 95). Along with leaders of the right-wing opposition, many leaders and activists of working-class movements were imprisoned and tortured.

CMSS thus began in a period where the overall policy context was friendlier to labour that the current neoliberal consensus, but the behaviour of the state was hostile and repressive. Despite its limitations, this background provided a better space for organising and building working class movements. There were a setback, downturn and scattering of the movement in the phase of liberalisation. A significant factor in these setbacks was the vacuum created by the murder of CMSS leader Shankar Guha Niyogi in 1991, linked with the failure of the union movement in India to respond strategically to liberalisation.

Debates in Indian Marxism: The Political Context of Niyogi's Thought

CMSS ideology closely connects to Niyogi, its paramount leader. As such it is necessary to understand Niyogi's ideological perspective to understand the genesis of CMSS. Niyogi joined the communist movement as a student activist in West Bengal during large-scale public unrest in 1959 in the food movement led by the Communist Party of India (CPI). A key event of his political radicalisation was the death of eighty people during police repression of a demonstration of workers and peasants against food shortages. After the split of the CPI in 1964, Niyogi joined the Communist Party of India-Marxist (CPIM). After the split in CPIM in 1967, he joined the All India Coordination Committee of Communist Revolutionaries (AICCCR), a platform of various communist groups that supported the Maoist movement after breaking with CPIM.

Niyogi joined the Communist Party of India (Marxist Leninist) (CPI(ML)) (India's first Maoist party) which was the result of a horizontal split in CPIM. CPIM's top leadership remained stable and united, and with some of its lower tiers of leadership, mainly grass root organisers and rank and file members, revolting and leaving CPIM. The essential nature of this split was rooted in a critique of CPIM's commitment to parliamentary socialism, and focus on electoral politics. This analysis favoured People's War against the Indian state and an argument that mass movement politics, or activities advocating reform, constituted revisionism, a betrayal of Marxism. This position excluded many left-wing critics of CPIM from participation in the new party, weakening the intellectual base of CPI(ML).

Several important debates emerged in the AICCCR, leading to the formation of the new party. The primary debates revolved around issues related to the method of struggle, namely the idea of people's war against the notion of mass movement politics, but there were also issues related to the understanding of the socio-economic structure of the society, possible class alliances and the nature of possible revolution in India. The dominant section of CPI(ML)'s leadership proceeded in haste, forming the party without resolving the debates; therefore, some of those groups and individuals who took up positions against People's War remained outside the new party. Without adequate resolution of these differences, the CPI(ML) split into various directions almost immediately after its formation (Singh 1987).

Niyogi would soon break with CPI(ML) based on their orientation toward People's War, with Niyogi supporting mass organisations and movements, finding himself expelled from CPI(ML) due to these differences (CMM 1992). Locating Niyogi's politics within the Indian left is necessary to understand the uniqueness of CMSS, which was a far more radical political formation than CPIM, but advocated a mass movement strategy against the Maoist idea of People's War.

No public positional statements were made by Niyogi while in CPI(ML). However, his experience within this party seems to have driven him toward independence from India's broader communist movement. While some of the splits in CPI(ML) created groups which strongly advocated mass movement politics and opposed People's War, rather than joining these, Niyogi worked independently, a critical decision in the formation of CMSS and critical to understanding its innovations in unionism. Niyogi never explicitly articulated his thoughts at that time. We are left to guess the exact reasons for his continued adherence to Marxism but independence from the Indian communist movement. The praxis of CMSS in Chhattisgarh demonstrates the difference in Niyogi's understanding of the problems of the communist movement.

Despite these differences, CMSS never attempted to theorise its experiences beyond the language of the mass movement itself. It never revisited its policies to theoretically articulate and present its differences from the other sections of the communist movement considering its experiences in Chhattisgarh. One of the significant failings of CMSS is its inability to enrich either its perspective or that of the communist movement in India. Despite having many capable organisers, CMSS could not develop a second generation of leadership. Niyogi remained the only accepted leader, with the strategy and tactics of the movement being an extension of his thought.

This problem can be seen in the inconsistency in CMSS literature when talking about Marxism and the mass movement. While articulating its views on Marxism and Communism, CMSS uses orthodox Marxist language (Niyogi 1991). Observing its mass movement on the ground, it confidently contributes new and creative Marxist ideas, without using Marxist terminology and without linking their thoughts to Marxist philosophy and debates in the Communist movement (see Sadgopal and Bahadur 1993).

Niyogi's Theory and Practice: A Critique of the Indian Left

Anti-capitalist working class movements must have an in-built aspect of transcending capitalism. From the working class' perspective, capitalism is not only capitalism but a struggle between capitalism and socialism. The working class must fight against the domination of capital and capture and create its space in all ideological, political, socio-cultural and economic spheres. In other words, the effort for building socialism starts within capitalism. In labour surplus societies like India, where capital is unable to absorb the economy and society entirely, and where much of the population survives as self-employed workers or in the reserve army of labour, this is of particular importance.

Unless a transition to socialism is imminent, without entering into a consistent struggle against the domination of capital, the working class movement cannot expand and cannot even survive as a socialist force for an extended period. Ultimately, this ends in empiricisation (Patnaik 2011), a departure from the broader task of transcending capitalism, or an acceptance of capitalist hegemony. The understanding of both the streams of the Indian communist movement—the parliamentary communists and non-parliamentary Marxist groups, reflects this problem. In simple terms, this argument articulates itself in a view that within capitalist society, it is not possible for political parties to go beyond capitalism. Even if they win power, they believe nothing is possible beyond the existing framework of capitalist democracy. Through this praxis, many left parties and unions have reduced themselves to being the left of capitalist politics in India.

Marxist-Leninist groups in India do not see capitalism as a struggle between capitalism and socialism and do not see the class struggle within capitalism as part of the fight for socialism. They believe the fight for socialism starts once the working class takes political power. Therefore, the task within capitalism revolves around organising the working class and raising its class consciousness. In this conception of politics, building alternative institutions with socialist perspectives is not part of their understanding.

The linear and determinist understanding of Marxism that prevails in the Indian communist movement supports a stage theory where the struggle for building socialism can only begin after capitalism is fully developed. The persistence of small production is considered pre-capitalist, and inherent in this understanding is that with capitalist expansion, small production will disappear. Struggles over small production are mostly not articulated as class struggles, and no strategic intervention appears for changing the fate of small economies either towards socialism or against capitalist expropriation.

Niyogi encountered these problems practically and developed an alternative model of working-class movement with inbuilt aspects of building socialism, beginning with capitalism. Niyogi did not articulate his strategy in existing Marxist terminology, and precisely due to this, he coined the new terms 'Sangharsh aur Nirman' (struggle and development) to explain his model. Some have incorrectly argued that Niyogi and CMSS 'transcended the Marxist framework' and reflected 'shift from a Marxist understanding of workers' exploitation' (Priyadarshi 2004). Niyogi's views, however, transcended the dominant linear understanding of Marxism.

The theory and practice of CMSS propose the philosophy of the working class is to destroy the old and exploitative socio-cultural, economic and political systems, and in its place, create new systems based on equality and respect for humanity. This aspect of destroying the old and creating the new must always be inbuilt in the strategy and day-to-day work of the working class movement. Without such a plan, class consciousness or socialist consciousness cannot develop among the working classes (see Niyogi's 1990 articles on the problems of trade union movement and various articles in Sangharsh aur Nirman [Sadgopal and Bahadur 1993]). In Marxist terminology, this is proposing that the struggle for building socialism must be inbuilt in the strategy and day-to-day work of the working class movement.

While developing the political orientation of CMSS, Niyogi proposed that workers' problems in workplace and society are linked. Thus, the working class movement should not restrict itself to workplace issues, and trade union work must extend beyond the workplace and work hours. Niyogi argued trade unions must have a class orientation and social orientation in their theory and practice. CMSS is, therefore, a forerunner to Social Movement Unionism. While authors such as Waterman (1993), Scipes (1992), Lambert (1990) and others have theorised this, the praxis of unions like CMSS significantly predates these theories.

On this basis, Niyogi proposed eighteen departments in the CMSS to define its areas of work, including the Trade Union, Work on Arrear and Fallback Wages, Peasants', Education, Savings, Health, Sports, Protection from Alcohol, Culture, Development of Workers' Slums, Women, Mess (The Kitchen of the Union), Construction, Legal, Library, Propaganda, Volunteers and Environment (Ganesh Chaudhari, Personal Communication, June 22, 2015). Later, CMM was formed as a political front of the union, and Mahila Mukti Morcha (Women's Liberation Front) was formed in 1980 (Ibid). CMSS also extended its work to students, and Chhattisgarh Students Federation was formed (Ibid).

The CMSS movement later established Shaheed Hospital as a working-class hospital, creating an institutional base within the community of Dalli-Rajhara. The movement also initiated mine workers' cooperatives and a farmers' cooperative. The movement took the initiative to develop irrigation infrastructure by constructing dams and wells in villages and built schools for workers' children. The anti-liquor movement, the movement for conservation of natural resources and workers' cultural movement were also initiatives worth mentioning. CMSS also published a weekly newspaper for workers named *Mitan*. In practice, the movement attempted to take the class struggle to all aspects of workers' lives, from the perspective of the struggle for building socialism, or Sangharsh aur Nirman.

The last thing to note in the ideological development of CMSS is the central role which Niyogi played as the movement's paramount thinker and strategist. Notwithstanding his positive qualities, Niyogi's experience in the Communist movement made him notoriously distrustful, even of, and perhaps especially of fellow labour activists (Sen 2014 Location 1417). Sen, a longtime activist who took part in the CMSS movement in the 1980s, noted that:

> as the union became established and was successful in securing economic gains for its members, the spontaneous stepping up of newer and newer worker comrades to share the workload of organization, as well as the participation of women, began to decline...at some point in the mid-1980s a freeze set in, and new leaders did not come up to any significant extent anymore. (Ibid, Loc 1416–7)

Niyogi had always played a significant role in the success of the union as a charismatic leader (Tucker 1968, p. 740) whose force of personality helped to break the ideological shackles of the previously accepted trade unionism, including the promotion of a democratic culture in union/cooperative politics. Sen's account demonstrates that over time CMSS political culture ossified, and the result was the over-centralisation of power in Niyogi's hands and lacking second-generation leaders.

Niyogi's role as a charismatic leader was a strength in the genesis of the movement and enabled it to deploy innovative strategies and rise quickly to power. Later in this chapter, this is also noted as a critical weakness of the movement. The decapitation strategy of assassinating Niyogi in 1991 was successful in engineering the downfall of the movement. The next sections will discuss some of the initiatives of CMSS and their significance, and the factors related to the decline of the movement after the murder of Niyogi.

The Mine Workers' Movement

The Struggle for Departmentalisation of Mines and Regularisation of Workers

The Dalli-Rajahara Mines directly serve the production of the Bhilai Steel Plant (BSP), a public sector unit headquartered in Bhilai, Chhattisgarh. Contractors ran the mines using contract mining labour, meaning workers had no direct employment relationship with BSP, exempting BSP from liability under India's labour laws. Until 1970 and even beyond in many industries like metal, mining and railways, it was common to outsource the activities down the production chain. A key demand of the working class movement, therefore, was to end the outsourcing system and establish direct employment with BSP.

In India, direct employees in public and private sectors experience better labour outcomes, particularly in larger enterprises. By contrast, contractors did not respect labour rights, an important issue underlying labour unrest during this period. The enactment of the Contract Labour (Regulation and Abolition) Act occurred in this background. The Act led to regularisation of a vast number of workers in metal industries, road transport, mines and railways, although not uniformly across India.

As the tendency towards liberalisation increased in the 1980s, a new wave of mechanisation, downsizing and contractualisation of labour occurred. Even when the law did not permit engaging contract labour in perennial activities (Government of India, Ministry of Labour 1970), many contract workers were still being engaged by companies, and struggles for the regularisation of employees suffered a significant setback. The focus of the CMSS-led mine workers' struggle was for departmentalisation of mines and regularisation of employees, a formalisation of both work and workforce.

Niyogi started working with the mine workers of Dalli-Rajhara in 1976–77. Until this point, AITUC was the dominant union of mine workers in the region. In the spring of 1977, contract workers revolted from AITUC and invited Niyogi to lead their movement (Ganesh Chaudhari, Personal Communication, June 22, 2015). Niyogi worked with mine workers in the region and was well known to them, having imprisoned for such activism during Indira Gandhi's emergency period, and recently released.

The catalyst for the workers' disaffection from AITUC was the union's handling of discrimination in annual bonus payments for India's Holi Festival (Ibid). The BSP management announced an Rs 308 bonus for departmentalised workers, and the contract workers demanded the same premium. BSP management announced an Rs 70 bonus for contract workers. Mineworkers' and CMSS leaders' accounts suggest acceptance of this differential payment as a principal reason for contract workers abandoning AITUC (Ibid). While this interpretation was denied by AITUC (Ibid), the contract workers saw the incident as a betrayal, which provoked their decision to abandon AITUC and form a separate union. The importance of the bonus issue was also highlighted by rival union leader Baldev Singh Man from AITUC who conceded that "after this issue, there was a definite split where the contract workers were with CMSS, and the regular workers were with us. (Baldev Singh Man, Personal Communication, 19 June 2015)."

The contract workers resigned from AITUC and started demonstrations to demand an equal bonus. At this point, Niyogi emerged as the leader of the Dalli-Rajhara mine workers' movement and on 3 March 1977, CMSS was formed (Ganesh Chaudhari, Personal Communication, June 22, 2015). CMSS demanded an equal bonus for contract workers along with an increase in daily wage, safety measures for mine workers and an increase in the pre-monsoon allowance for hut repairs (Ibid). Two months later, CMSS launched a strike for these demands lasting twenty-two days. The police arrested Niyogi during this strike on 1 June 1977, and the next day workers organised a demonstration demanding his release (Ibid).

During this demonstration, eleven workers died due to police repression, and hundreds of others were seriously injured. A memorial erected in front of the CMSS office and the name of the hospital built by the workers' movement, Shaheed Hospital (Martyrs' Hospital), commemorates these workers. The eventual outcome of the strike was a partial victory for the workers. Niyogi was released, the BSP management accepted a bonus payment of Rs100 to contract workers, and increased the pre-monsoon hut repair allowance from Rs20 to Rs100 (Ibid). Most importantly, despite CMSS not being a recognised union, BSP management made a significant agreement with it on the issue of fall back wages, an argument that seasonally non-utilised contract workers should be entitled to a maintenance stipend (Ibid). BSP management constituted a committee to fix the norm for fall back wages, and workers' representatives were also included (Ibid), winning the union legitimacy as the representative of contract mine workers.

After that, the focus of CMSS was on departmentalisation and regularisation of workers and the issue of fall back wages. The demand for departmentalisation was not new and was taken up previously by the AITUC-led union of mine workers, Samyukt Khadan Mazdoor Sangh (SKMS). Before CMSS emerged in 1977, the first phase of departmentalisation was complete with 3374 workers departmentalised. As such, there is continuity in some if not all of the strategies and tactics of CMSS and AITUC. Both saw the state as a potential partner regarding guaranteeing employment for its members.

Nair (2011, p. 178) has argued that in the 1970s and early 1980s, CMSS encountered the state which despite its limitations 'acknowledged the role of citizens as labourers' and thus 'provided a platform for them to struggle and resist'. Many trade unions in India during this period, therefore, constructed state-centric strategies for improving members' conditions, a strategy that collapsed as India shifted to neoliberalism, and the state withdrew from managing the economy and guaranteeing the welfare of its citizens.

The development of cooperatives came about in part due to the willingness of CMSS to experiment with new strategies and tactics. However, it also should be seen in the broader economic and political context. The enactment of the Contract Labour (Regulation and Abolition) Act 1970 forced contractors to follow specific labour standards and provide facilities like canteens, drinking water, latrines and first-aid (Government of India, Ministry of Labour 1970), causing rising costs and decreasing profits. Additionally, profitability in some regions of mining was declining. With contractors discontinuing operations in response to this, there was space for cooperatives of mine workers to take over with little opposition.

The strengthened position of the mine workers and their unions forced BSP management to departmentalise a section of the mine workers. Some mines were then directly controlled by BSP to maintain a supply of raw materials. This same situation facilitated the development of mine workers' cooperatives, discussed in the next section. The departmentalisation of these workers created a division between contract and departmentalised workers (Lin 1992). AITUC was not able to integrate the issues of contract workers and was more oriented toward the departmentalised workers, creating space for a new union of contract workers to emerge.

CMSS was also unable to unite the regular, departmental and contract workers. By and large, it remained the union of contract workers, to some extent representing departmentalised workers who emerged from its ranks. Regular workers and most departmentalised workers stayed in AITUC. The regular workers were workers who had come from other parts of India, whereas most contract workers and those later departmentalised were Adivasis, and this focus would remain an essential part of CMSS's politics.

While the demand for departmentalisation and regularisation of workers was not new, the understanding and approach of CMSS were. As Ganesh Chaudhari of CMSS argued, "the natural resources belonged to the Adivasis, that exploitation of the land led to the destruction of their livelihoods and environment, and that it did not provide decent employment to the workers" (Ganesh Chaudhari, Personal Communication, June 22, 2015). "Therefore, workers should be compensated through regular jobs in BSP for this destruction and displacement" (Ibid). In 1979 CMSS presented a demand charter to BSP management with eighteen demands, including departmentalisation of mines and the absorption of all workers as regular workers of BSP. At that time, BSP was planning to mechanise mine operations and downsize the workforce (Ibid). The primary challenge for CMSS and the mine workers was that BSP management accepted the minor demands but rejected departmentalisation and regularisation of contract workers.

CMSS continued to argue for the rights of workers to regular jobs but realised without satisfying management with an alternative plan to increase productivity; it was hard to win this demand. CMSS managed to get the support of some experts and conducted a study to propose an alternative to complete mechanisation. A convincing plan of semi-mechanisation was prepared that offered efficiency and space for retaining the workforce.

Management accepted the plan, and 2000 workers were absorbed as BSP workers in the same mine with 2000 others transferred to other mines without any retrenchment. BSP management continued to argue for full mechanisation, the rift between CMSS and management was growing, but the semi-mechanisation agreement appeared to buy them time. In 1980, BSP, CMSS and the contractors signed a tripartite agreement for only partial departmentalisation and a small wage increase.

In 1985–86, BSP management attempted to use machines to load waste ore, replacing the manual loading process and the manual loading workers. CMSS successfully opposed and stopped this. In 1989, BSP drastically increased the production targets, which increased the workload of mine workers to unacceptable levels as part of a strategy to pressurise acceptance of complete mechanisation and a downsizing of the workforce. The workers protested and faced police repression in response. BSP management offered a Voluntary Retirement Scheme (VRS) where departmentalised workers were offered redundancy packages in exchange for a termination of employment, as part of their strategy to mechanise.

The increased workload, coupled with the VRS offer, led many departmentalised workers to accept VRS and leave their jobs, which resulted in a decline in union influence. During this period, CMSS spread in broader industrial areas of Chhattisgarh, particularly around Bhilai. An active movement of contract workers emerged in Bhilai industries, with CMSS attempting to counter declining influence in the mines by expanding into other areas and industries. Niyogi's assassination occurred in 1991, during this movement. Just after the murder of Niyogi, the management implemented the VRS scheme on a large scale. "Approximately 1,300 people opted for VRS and left their jobs at the mines" remembers Durga Prasad, former BSP worker and CMSS treasurer, revealing the impact which the VRS scheme had on the union (Durga Prasad, Personal Communication, 21 June 2015).

Many departmentalised workers were choosing to utilise VRS and lost their connection to the Union. The VRS strategy weakened CMSS and Niyogi's assassination compounded this. While interviewed workers, union and party leaders attributed great significance to the Niyogi assassination in explaining the decline of the union, the truth was that Niyogi was partly responsible. Centralisation of power around Niyogi and his almost single-handed control over the ideological and strategic aspects of the union meant no second-generation leaders were in place to take over this role. The next generation of leaders was exposed and unable to understand how to deal with the problematic situation. At the time when the movement needed to mobilise workers to contest mechanisation and the BSP's VRS strategy, the union found itself in disarray.

In 1994, BSP made an in-principle agreement with CMSS for departmentalisation of all workers, including those working under contractors and in cooperative societies. Unlike earlier agreements, there was no provision for regularisation of workers; the departmentalised workers would remain 'departmentalised' until retirement, a midway position between a contract worker and a regular worker. BSP management finally implemented this program in 1996. There was some opposition from a section of CMSS leadership against this agreement, and the unionists opposed to the deal left the movement, weakening it further.

BSP management reached a position where they could use natural attrition to deunionise the mines and banned recruitment of new workers. The departmentalisation without benefits of regularisation proved an easy way to buy off workers and eliminate the union presence. A significant section of the departmentalised workers soon reached retirement age, and another large part opted for VRS, thus reducing both workforce and union presence drastically. While many of the individual workers benefited from this, it was a massive loss for the community as employment opportunities for the local Adivasi communities disappeared.

Departmentalisation only helped workers who fulfilled certain conditions which were part of a deliberate attempt to downsize. The conditions included being: (a) registered in contractors or cooperative societies before 1975; (b) below fifty years of age; and (c) medically fit. Workers not on an employment roll or those who had begun work more recently, had their jobs terminated. Workers older than fifty could work up to fifty-eight years of age but were not departmentalised and thus enjoyed no retirement or other benefits.

After departmentalization there had remained about 5000 workers, which included 2500 departmentalised plus regular workers and 2500 contract workers and cooperative society workers. Natural attrition from VRS further reduced the workforce. In 2015, the total workforce was approximately 3200, including about 1700 regular plus departmentalised workers, 1200 contract workers and 300 cooperative society workers. By comparison, the total workforce in Dalli-Rajhara Mines in 1980 was about 18,000, with 8000 contract workers. The overall strength of contract workers was reduced to about 1200, weakening CMSS' base.

CMSS organisational logic had revolved around the issues of contract workers. However, their base increasingly became split between departmentalised former contract workers and the remnants of the contract system. CMSS needed to rebuild its base among departmentalised and regular workers, articulate their issues to integrate them into the broader CMSS movement and lead the collective bargaining process. With liberalisation negatively changing the policy environment, and with the loss of leadership, CMSS was not able to address this task. The organising of regular workers was still primarily led by AITUC, but the workers were dissatisfied with this union as well.

An example which demonstrates the ability of new unions to organise, and the opportunities missed by CMSS, can be seen during this phase. The Communist Party of India (Marxist)–led Centre for Indian Trade Unions (CITU) entered the scene in 1996 and gradually captured this space. In 2013, in a BSP election determining which bargaining agent would represent the mines, CITU won an absolute majority of departmentalized and regularised workers (1400/2500). On paper, AITUC and CMSS dominated the regular and departmentalised workers in membership numbers; however, in the election, many workers, including their members, voted for CITU, with CMSS getting only 89 out of 2500 votes. Long-time CMSS activist Shankhu Ram commented that "CMSS members defected and voted for CITU, we can confirm this because none of the other unions lost their previous vote share, only CMSS did" (Shankhu Ram, Personal Communication, 15 June 2015).

The Cooperatives of Mine Workers

As discussed, the implementation of the Contract Workers (Abolition and Regulation) Act 1970, increased contractors operating costs leading some contractors to discontinue operations creating space for +mineworkers' cooperatives. An obscure colonial law, the Cooperative Societies Act, 1912, allows workers to form cooperatives in India, by registering with a state government registrar, based on mutual economic interest (Government of India, Legislative Department 2017). From a legal standpoint, members of a cooperative society have equal rights regarding employment, the distribution of profits, and the election of office bearers.

As contractors began to withdraw from Dalli-Rajhara due to declining profitability, cooperative formation helped maintain employment options for workers. The Congress Party of India affiliated All India Trade Union Congress (AITUC) ran three. Apart from these societies, there were three to four larger contractors engaging the rest of the workforce. Worker cooperatives and a dwindling number of private contractors employed by a government-run public sector unit in the Bhilai Steel Plant constituted the overall dynamic of the mines.

As the contractors withdrew from Dalli-Rajhara, the workers were led by their trade unions to form cooperative societies and take over the work they previously performed. Committees of cooperative societies have been trained by workers to supervise and execute work, and trade unions (INTUC and AITUC) controlled and led this process. Each cooperative society had several hundred members who elected the office bearers of the societies, and the cooperatives were relatively autonomous, except for the mandatory government registrar who was attached to each cooperative society. At this point, office bearers tended to be the union leaders from either INTUC or AITUC.

The workers were in a better condition than under the contractors; however, there was no significant change in working conditions or wages. Puna Ram, who had been employed in one of the cooperative societies during the time, noted that "there was not much difference between cooperative and contract work, the main difference was the surplus was in the hands of the cooperative societies, but our salaries and living standard remained the same. What happened to the profits depended on the leaders: Some union leaders were corrupt and would appropriate the profits, otherwise would seek permission from the government to distribute the profits" (Puna Ram, Personal Communication, 15 June 2015). INTUC and AITUC had philosophies of trade unionism which led them to focus on the permanent, formalised section of the workforce. Union activists from AITUC and INTUC would seek to become office bearers of cooperative societies primarily for the personal benefits or to bolster their CV, and their later removal as a result of the contract workers' revolt had no noticeable legacy effects.

During this period the workers were not made aware of contract terms, and there was no formal system of profit sharing. The union leaders were controlling these societies without any real control exercised by the workers. This changed with the entry of CMSS onto the political scene. "When CMSS was formed, almost all workers under contractors and most of the cooperative societies left their previous unions and joined CMSS, because of its focus on the issues of contract workers" (Ibid). This gave CMSS effective control over the cooperative societies.

CMSS tapped the heightened political consciousness of the contract workers and utilised the cooperatives as a valuable recruiting ground and source of political power within the Dalli-Rajhara Mines. "After the workers revolted and we gained control over most of the cooperative societies, we established a closed shop situation over time whereby to join the cooperative societies you needed to be a member of CMSS" (Ganesh Chaudhari, Personal Communication, June 22, 2015). Not only did the union grow in strength because of this, but it gained a critical leverage point in the labour-intensive activities of the mine, making their threats of industrial action more effective.

Under CMSS the cooperatives developed as democratic institutions. CMSS restructured the cooperative giving workers' committees full control to run the cooperatives. At this point, they became aware of the terms and contracts and other aspects like additional facilities and payments provided by BSP for running cooperative affairs. The workers thus became equipped for collective bargaining. Ganesh Chaudhury remembers that "We signed the contracts, reworked plans given by BSP supervisors and engineers, built teams and executed the work. We were also able to research ways to improve efficiency and decrease stress without using any new technology" (Ganesh Chaudhari, Personal Communication, June 22, 2015).

CMSS took initiatives to improve occupational health and safety standards and promoted equal profit sharing improving the working conditions and earnings of workers significantly (Ibid). "We were able to gain control of the cooperatives which meant for the first time we were able to share the profits with the workers. The government only permitted 25% profit sharing, but we used some tricks to avoid this restriction, for example by giving in-kind gifts to workers. All of this improved our standard of living" (Ibid). The cooperative dynamics also exerted pressure on contractors to improve working conditions and earnings of workers outside the cooperatives.

Improvement of working conditions emerged as a major focus of cooperatives under CMSS. Safe drinking water was a significant problem and workers depended on untreated stream water. Under CMSS cooperatives managed to bring water tankers to provide safe drinking water to workers. Societies also purchased various new implements that were more effective and safer. One of the CMSS organisers recalled that "CMSS changed the objectives of the cooperative somewhat to emphasize working conditions and safety, this meant bringing water via tankers, and purchasing more effective tools" (Ibid).

With increasing conflicts between CMSS with BSP management, cooperative societies also faced problems, including problems engineered by the state. The engineering of a crisis for one of the major cooperative societies occurred in 1981 whose election was due after its managing committee reached its tenure of three years. For various reasons, it was late in completing the election. The government of India's Director of Societies took action on this pretext and suspended the power of the society's president and secretary. The result of this was to block all transactions made with society funds. This was "a continuing measure to crush the CMSS and replace it with either AITUC (run by the Communist Party of India) or INTUC (run by the Indian National Congress) whose political affiliations were close to the government of the day" (Chaita Ram, Personal Communication, 14 June 2015) per Chaita Ram who was one of the union office bearers at the time. After a long struggle, the rights of the society were restored; however, the message of hostility from the government was clear.

There was also consistent pressure from BSP for mechanisation of mine operations and a ban on recruitment of new workers as their payment to the societies and contractors was made based on workers engaged and the work done. After the retirement of any workers, no new recruitment was allowed, and therefore the workload increased. It was this situation that led to an increase in informal hiring practices, with many new workers hired in the second half of the 1980s but not registered on the payroll. When the last departmentalisation happened, it was these workers who lost their jobs.

In the last departmentalisation in 1996, departmentalised workers were not allowed future regularisation. All cooperative societies dissolved upon departmentalisation of workers. In this way, the whole experiment of cooperative societies came to an end.

Conclusion

Niyogi's assassination in 1991 created a vacuum regarding any alternate accepted leadership. Many differences emerged among second-tier leaders and by 1994–95 CMSS had split into four organisations, reducing its power drastically (Kerswell and Pratap, Field Notes, June 20, 2015). In the phase of globalisation and liberalisation the whole politico-economic environment changed, and in the absence of any compelling political leadership, the organisations were not able to devise new strategies to sustain and develop the movement. The drastic downsizing of the mines reduced the strength of mine workers. These factors led to the decline of the movement.

The rise of CMSS marks a unique part of India's labour history. Objective factors such as the political environment are only a partial explanation for the rise of CMSS. We have argued that subjective factors, such as the willingness of CMSS leaders to be innovators regarding their ideological position, but also regarding their strategy and tactics of trade unionism, both of which gave the union significant legitimacy with contract workers. The result of this was CMSS's rapid rise in power and influence, the construction of enduring workers' institutions such as the Shaheed Hospital and the development of socialist systems within a capitalist economy such as the mineworkers' cooperatives.

However, it is unavoidable to say that the movement has faced a significant decline. Once a leading militant union in India, in the words of Nair (2011, p. 177) it has been 'reduced to a routine client in court'. Several factors explain the decline of CMSS. Again, while the external environment took a turn for the worse with the advent of liberalisation in India, internal weaknesses of the movement were the primary explanatory causes for the movement's fall. While Niyogi's role as a charismatic leader played a decisive role in the union's history, the over centralisation of power in his was a critical weakness that prevented the development of a new generation of leaders and led to the splintering of the movement upon his assassination.

Despite innovating workers' institutions within capitalism, the movement relied too heavily on the Indian state to resolve their grievances through 'departmentalisation', a strategy that was common in the Indian union movement during the Nehruvian socialist period. When the state was no longer a willing partner, this approach led to the collapse of the union's power. While CMSS methods predated social movement unionism significantly, the inability of the movement to theorise their experiences is a significant shortcoming and a missed opportunity both for trade unionists in India but also globally, and for the Marxist movement in general.

Beyond the Workplace: The Legacy of CMSS

We have stressed that one of the critical factors that allowed CMSS to stand apart from the Indian trade union movement was its social movement union orientation. Thus far we have focused on the role of cooperatives. However, the union through its political arm CMM was involved in many other areas of public life as well. While it is not possible to document each of these in detail, some of the union's achievements in this regard include the establishment of Shaheed Hospital and a Public Health Movement, the development of a social and cultural movement, the development of a peasant collective farming movement and the development of people's technology.

The most important achievement of the movement has been in public health. A major problem that contract workers faced was their ineligibility to use the BSP hospital, as they were not considered direct employees of BSP. The contractors and cooperative societies used facilities of various private hospitals on a case by case basis, meaning a general lack of regular health care and the absence of medical insurance for workers and their families.

CMM was able to build a full-fledged hospital in Dalli-Rajahara in 1981–82. This was done entirely by the cooperative efforts of the workers. The major financial contribution came from mine workers' cooperatives, and other workers in the region and the hospital's construction work were entirely done by the mine workers. Chaita Ram, the Vice President of one of the cooperative societies, remembered: "Both the union and the cooperative society contributed funds to the hospital and helped to construct it, donating fixtures and fittings. CMM constructed the hospital without the use of wage labour. Volunteers contributed trucks and materials. Only some materials like bricks and glass were purchased. Each month the societies would contribute some money to the hospital as an allowance. Each worker would contribute about 130rs per month, of an approximate salary of 400-500rs" (Chaita Ram, Personal Communication, 14 June 2015). This has now developed into a 40-bed double story hospital with all relevant facilities and workers of the region felt proud of their hospital during interviews.

In a country without a socialised health system, this hospital provides affordable treatment and integrates treatment with health education. Doctors and nurses in the hospital were initially supporters of the movement and mainly the product of the revolutionary student movement in West Bengal. The decline of CMSS has had no significant impact on the hospital and public health movement which remains an enduring legacy of CMSS in Dalli-Rajhara.

CMSS also built a strong peasant movement through CMM. Along with fighting against various injustices, CMM mobilised peasants to create cooperative irrigation infrastructure and introduced innovative cultivation methods to increase yields. The leader of CMM, Janaklal Thakur, was also elected as a member of Madhya Pradesh Legislative assembly. An additional lasting impact of the CMM movement is on village level government in the region. CMM contests, and at times wins, some village panchayat elections.

A notable example of a way that CMM developed a collective method of living and working can be seen in the village of Banjari, a neighbouring village of Dalli-Rajhara. In 1978, the Kharkhara Dam project, built to facilitate the Bhilai Steel Plant, displaced the entire village and submerged its farming land. There was no resettlement package provided by any level of government, and no compensation was paid to the villagers.

CMM assisted the displaced farmers, aiding the villagers. They identified a new area of forest to develop farming land. Following this, CMM mobilised the villagers to occupy a 60-acre section of the State Forest and began developing it. This involved a struggle against the Indian State, and specifically the Forestry Department, as the land was part of a state forest. After a protracted struggle, the Forestry Department permitted the villagers to cultivate the land without any transference of land title. This creates particular limitations on the viability of the farming venture, as infrastructural improvements such as tube wells cannot be constructed as the land is not owned by the villagers.

The most interesting part of the land venture concerns the dynamics of cultivation which were developed. Under the leadership of CMM, the villagers agreed to cultivate the land collectively rather than subdivide it among the individual households. In the previous village before displacement, the land was farmed individually by households, and thus CMM can be seen to have significantly impacted the farming methods of the village. All of the work of the village is done collectively, and decisions about the village are made collectively according to democratic methods.

The villagers face an ongoing struggle with the government to improve their living conditions. The central focus of their struggle is for land tenure, which would not only give the villagers a permanent connection with the land but would also enable the land to be upgraded by constructing infrastructure. Nonetheless, Banjari village is just one of many examples whereby CMM responded to a crisis innovatively and created a collective response.

CMM also evolved an understanding that technology is also an arena of class struggle, and thereby invested effort into "people's technology". Technological development means mechanisation and labour replacing technology, often also destroying nature. CMSS activists argued there can also be technology that eases efforts of labour and takes care of nature and environment. The Shaheed Garage at Dalli-Rajahara created by cooperative efforts of the workers was CMSS' experiment in this direction. There were plans to expand the garage into an industrial training institute or polytechnic college which were derailed by the decline of the movement.

CMM started working on the technological front around 1982 when 70 mechanics of various garages in Dalli-Rajhara struck for better working conditions resulting in the retrenchment of 40 workers. CMM opened a cooperative garage with these workers to start the technological enterprises of CMM movement and named it Shaheed (Martyrs) Garage. Along with the regular business, the garage was established as a centre to impart technical knowledge to mechanics, who had the skills to repair engines but knew nothing about the science behind them.

Interviews with workers suggested the cooperative garage was a successful enterprise, and mainly worked to repair the trucks working in the mines. It contributed an average of Rs2500 per month to the union in profits during the 1980s. With the guidance of some engineer friends, it also developed into a teaching and learning centre which allowed for the development of people's technology.

Each of these examples is further evidence that both the theory and practice of CMSS/CMM was oriented toward actively creating collective ways of living and working. While this began in the cooperative societies of Dalli-Rajhara, the legacy of CMM and Niyogi is undoubtedly one of being great innovators regarding developing radical collective institutions as building blocks toward socialism.

References

Agarwala, Rina. 2013. *Informal Labor, Formal Politics and Dignified Discontent in India*. New York: Cambridge University Press.

Chaudhury, Saumitra. 1977. Nationalisation of Oil Companies in India. *Economic and Political Weekly*. Vol. 12, Issue No. 10, 05 Mar, 1977

CMM. 1992. *Zameen par khade rahkar jinhone aasman chhua (Those who reached the sky by standing on the ground)*. Lok Sahitya Parishad (People's Literature Council): Dalli-Rajahara, Chhattisgarh.

Fantasia, Rick. 1988. *Cultures of Solidarity: Consciousness, Action and Contemporary American Workers*. Berkeley, CA: University of California Press.

Government of India, Labour Bureau. 2007. *Report on Socio-Economic Conditions of Scheduled Tribes Labour at Vapi, Valsad, Navsari and Sachin (Gujarat) 2006–7*. Available from: http://labourbureau.nic.in/SE_Gujarat%2006-07_Contents.htm [Online], p6

Government of India, Legislative Department. *The Cooperative Societies Act 1912*. Available from: http://indiacode.nic.in/qryactyear2.asp?txtact=1912&submit1=Submit [Online], 2017.

Government of India, Ministry of Labour. *The Contract Labour (Regulation and Abolition) Act 1970*. Available from: http://labour.bih.nic.in/Acts/contract_labour_regulation_and_abolition_act_1970.pdf [Online], 1970.

Hensman, Rohini. 2011. *Workers, Unions and Global Capitalism: Lessons from India*. New York: Columbia University Press.

Kendall, Diana. 2005. *Sociology in our Times*. Thomson Wadsworth: Stamford.

Lambert, Robert. 1990. Kilusang Mayo Uno & the Rise of Social Movement Unionism in the Philippines. *Labour & Industry: A Journal of the Social and Economic Relations of Work* 3, no. 2–3: 258–80.

Lin, Sharat G. 1992. Shankar Guha Niyogi: Beyond Conventional Trade Unionism in India. *Bulletin of Concerned Asia Scholars*. Vol 24, no. 3: 16–25.

Malik, Yogendra Kumar. 1988. India: The Years of Indira Gandhi. Leiden: Brill Publishers.

McAdam, Doug, Tarrow, Sidney and Tilly, Charles. 1996. *Towards an Integrated Perspective on Social Movements and Revolution*. Available from: http://media.library.ku.edu.tr/reserve/resspring07/soci304_myuksel/week10.pdf

McCarthy, John and Zald, Mayer. 1977. Resource Mobilization and Social Movements: A Partial Theory. *American Journal of Sociology*, Vol 82 Iss 6: 1212–1241.

McCarthy, John and Zald, Mayer. 2002. The Enduring Vitality of the Resource Mobilization Theory of Social Movements. In, Turner, Jonathan. *Handbook of Sociological Theory*. Plenum Publishers: New York.

Menon, Nivedita and Nigam, Aditya. 2007. *Power and Contestation: India Since 1989*. Zed Books: London.

Moody, Kim. 2002 Towards an international social-movement unionism. *Industrial Relations: Labour Markets, Labour Process and Trade Unionism*. Vol 2, 418.

Nair, Manjusha. 2011. Differences in Workers' Narratives of Contention in Two Central Indian Towns. *International Labor and Working Class History* Vol 19: 175–194.

Niyogi, Shankar Guha. 1990. *Bharat ke Trade Union Andolan ki Samsyaen* (Challenges Facing the Trade Union Movement in India). Lok Sahitya Parishad (People's Literature Council), CMM, Dalli-Rajahara, Chhattisgarh.

Niyogi, Shankar Guha. 1991. *Principles of Marxism*. Shramjeevi Swasthha Udyog (Workers' Health Centre).

Palmer, Norman. 1976. India in 1975: Democracy in Eclipse. *Asian Survey*. Vol 16, No 2, 95–110.

Parry, Jonathan. 2003. Nehru's Dream and the Village 'Waiting Room': Long-distance Labour Migrants to a Central Indian Steel Town. *Contributions to Indian Sociology*. Vol 37, Iss 1.

Parry, Jonathan. 2008. The Sacrifices of Modernity in a Soviet-built Steel Town in Central India. In, Pine, Frances and de Pina-Cabral, João. On the Margins of Religion. Berghahn Books: New York.

Patnaik, Prabhat. 2011. The Left in Decline. *Economic and Political Weekly*, July.

Priyadarshi, Praveen. 2004. *The Chhattisgarh Mukti Morcha: A Case Study CHHATTISGARH.* http://planningcommission.nic.in/reports/sereport/ser/seeds/seed_mvmt.pdf

Rosenthal, Naomi B. and Michael Schwartz. 1989. Spontaneity and Democracy in Social Movements. pp. 33–60 in Klandermans, B (Ed). *Organizing for Change: Social Movement Organization in Europe and the United States.* Greenwich, CT: JAI Press.

Sadgopal, Anil, and Shyam Bahadur. 1993. *Sangharsh aur Nirman* (Struggle and Development). New Delhi: Rajkamal Prakashan.

Scipes, Kim. 1992. Understanding the New Labor Movements in the 'Third World': The Emergence of Social Movement Unionism. *Critical Sociology* Vol 19, no. 2: 81–101.

Seidman, Gay. 1994. *Manufacturing Militance: Workers' Movements in Brazil and South Africa, 1970–1985.* Berkeley and Los Angeles: University of California Press.

Sen, Ilina. 2014. Inside Chhattisgarh: A Political Memoir. Penguin: Gurgaon. (Digital Edition)

Singh, Chandrika. 1987. *Communist and Socialist Movement in India—A Critical Account.* Delhi: Mittal Publications.

Tilly, Charles. 1977. *From Mobilization to Revolution.* CSRO Working Paper #156.

Tucker, Robert. 1968. The Theory of Charismatic Leadership. *Daedelus.* Vol 97, No 3.

Waterman, P. 1993. Social-Movement Unionism: A New Union Model for a New World Order? *Review*, Vol 16, Iss 3: 245–278.

Zald, Mayer. 2000. Ideologically Structured Action: An Enlarged Agenda for Social Movement Research. *Mobilizations.* Vol 5, Iss 1.

CHAPTER 4

The Alcond Employees Industrial Co-Operative Society Limited

Introduction

In this chapter, we will present a case study of the Alcond Employees Industrial Co-Operative Society Ltd. (Alcond Cooperative henceforth), a wire factory owned and run by workers in Kolkata, West Bengal, India. The Alcond Cooperative is an industrial cooperative, in that the workers manage a capital-intensive production process. From the Alcond case, we hope to learn lessons about the formation of industrial cooperatives and their unique challenges.

There are some essential contextual matters to present when considering the Alcond Cooperative case. Firstly, the creation of industrial cooperatives in India exists in the context of factory closures and the responses by labour organisations. Here, we observe that industrial cooperatives in India have been defensive, responding to the trend of factory closures as opposed to a more proactive model of cooperative formation as has been seen in other countries. We find that across the mainstream political perspectives in India, from the Hindu nationalist and Bharatiya Mazdoor Sangh (BMS) to the Centre for Indian Trade Unions (affiliated with the Communist Party of India (Marxist)), each organisation has been limited to a defensive view of cooperatives. In this chapter, we aim to explore why this is the case.

To ground our analysis of the Alcond Cooperative in its local context, we will also discuss the specific nature of the economic conditions of West Bengal. We begin with a brief overview of the economic structure of West

T. Kerswell, S. Pratap, *Worker Cooperatives in India*,
https://doi.org/10.1007/978-981-13-0384-5_4

Bengal as well as a discussion of capital flight as a critical trend that impacted the province and helped generate a process of cooperative formation. We will also discuss the history and ideology of the Communist Party of India (Marxist) (CPIM henceforth), the political party that governed the province from 1977 to 2011 and was the longest democratically elected Marxist provincial governments in the world. The CPIM played a significant role in the Alcond Cooperative's history, not just as the governing party, but by its Centre for Indian Trade Unions (CITU henceforth) forming, initiating and running the Alcond Cooperative.

Following this, there will be a discussion of the history, formation and management of the Alcond Cooperative. In this section, we will consider the structure of the organisation and how it makes decisions. We will also discuss the technical aspects of the Alcond Cooperative's work, what types of materials the factory produces, and where the factory sits in the overall structure of production in India. Finally, in this section, we will consider the impact of cooperative formation on the pay and conditions of Alcond Cooperative's workers.

Sadly, the Alcond Cooperative has encountered trouble in its recent history, notably since the implementation of neoliberal economic reform in India since 1994, and then after the defeat of the CPI-M led Left Front in the 2011 elections. A discussion of the pitfalls that the Alcond Cooperative has faced is an integral part of working-class history in West Bengal and India. These experiences also shed light on the limitations of the cooperative model behind Alcond. We can call this model "union-led state-assisted cooperatives" due to the massive influence and dependence on specific regulatory, political, and material assistance from the Left Front government in West Bengal. The Left Front, in turn, was intimately connected to the trade union operating the cooperative under Leninist principles of the relation between the Communist Party and the trade unions. As we will see, however, there were severe limitations regarding the assistance provided by the Left Front to the Alcond Cooperative. While the Alcond Cooperative saw themselves as politically and economically dependent on the Left Front, the reality of the situation was that they received insufficient assistance and at times were subject to measures from the government that actively harmed the cooperative.

The chapter will conclude with a statement of the lessons that we can learn from the Alcond cooperative. We feel that Alcond is an example of how workers can own and run a factory that produces highly technical materials and relatively capital-intensive processes. The case did, however, demonstrate some weaknesses, some objective and some subjective. Regarding the material weaknesses of industrial cooperatives, they appear to be the result of the merging of industrial and financial capital. The Alcond Cooperative found itself progressively frozen out of the financial system and dependent on political favours and its skills base to maintain itself. This problem would be likely to replicate itself in many situations where workers have the necessary skills but not the necessary capital. This is a significant question that the trade union movement would need to think through to address this problem with industrial cooperatives.

Regarding the subjective factors, the lack of a proactive, cooperative building strategy between CITU and CPIM limited Alcond. Following a mostly defensive approach to cooperative formation, the Alcond Cooperative and other cooperatives in India have been able to preserve employment and an industrial base at least for some time. This example, however, compares poorly against, for instance, the Mondragon Cooperative movement in the Basque region, which pursued a proactive, cooperative strategy and was thus able to maintain itself as a movement successfully to this day.

Whatever the limitations of the Alcond Cooperative model and whatever will happen to the Alcond Cooperative in the future, it deserves a celebration as a grand social experiment, a shining example to the power of workers to organise and manage a complicated production process in a hostile environment. This chapter is therefore also a celebration of the decades of achievement of the Alcond Cooperative workers.

To support this case study, we undertook semi-structured interviews with a number of the Alcond Cooperative workers and the worker-leaders as part of a series of site visits conducted in 2015. The Alcond Cooperative employees and leaders were able to give us a detailed account of the history of the Alcond Cooperative, of the technical matters relating to its day-to-day existence, the structure of the organisation, and the problems it faced.

It is notable that all of the Alcond Cooperative workers are both members of CITU as well as CPIM, and this helped us to understand the connections between the cooperative, the union, and the party. In addition to this, we interviewed one of CITU's regional coordinators for cooperative enterprises in order to corroborate our findings. We selected interview participants via chain referral sampling.

Cooperative Formation: A Response to Capital Flight

A critical factor to understand regarding the formation of the Alcond Cooperative is the backdrop of economic change in West Bengal, as well as the overall economic picture of India at the time of cooperative formation. In this section, we will document the history of capital flight in West Bengal by describing the context in which the formation of the Alcond Cooperative occurred. We will also highlight the economic context of post-liberalization India and, in particular, post-liberalization West Bengal to obtain a greater understanding of the circumstances of the decline of the Alcond Cooperative.

Historically, West Bengal has been one of the leading industrial provinces of India. Before colonisation by the British, the province was significantly developed as a manufacturing centre and had to be actively deindustrialized to ensure the dominance of the British industry based on a classical Prebischian dependency model of India exporting raw materials and importing manufactured goods. In this section, we will see that deindustrialization is a theme in West Bengal to which the Left Front government and the Alcond Cooperative were a response. While deindustrialization is often associated with the Left Front government's rule, its history is far longer than this.

Before British colonisation, West Bengal was one of the most advanced industrial regions in India. Britain forcibly deindustrialized West Bengal, the first part of India that was colonised by Britain, and yet made no investments in agriculture, creating an enormous economic crisis in Bengal where both industry and agriculture faced simultaneous stagnation (Patnaik 2006, pp. 492–3). This history of exploitation was then compounded by Britain's use of India to finance its war against Japan, which while impacting India as a whole, disproportionately impacted West Bengal through the Bengal famine, leading to approximately three million deaths and the total impoverishment of a further 500,000 people (ibid, p. 493).

Despite this long history of ruin, when India gained independence in 1947, West Bengal was India's most affluent province along with Maharashtra (Lahiri and Yi 2004, p. 1). This often-quoted statistic, however, masked a mire of social contradictions. By far, the most significant industry in West Bengal was the jute industry. The biggest problem with this is that Partition significantly impacted this industry. While the majority of the jute factories were in and around Kolkata, the majority of the jute plantations were now in East Pakistan (now Bangladesh) (Ray 2011, p. 4).

The development of a new engineering industry encouraged by India's first five-year plan compensated somewhat for this and this economic history is part of the reason for The Alcond Cooperative's existence (Ray 2011, p. 5; Patnaik 2011).

The revival in West Bengal's fortunes would, however, be short-lived. India experienced its first post-independence economic crisis as a result of the 1965 war with Pakistan, which led to a significant reduction in public investment. The railways budget which in 1964–1965 was approximately 2,700,000,000 rupees, but in 1966–1967 declined to approximately 1,600,000,000 rupees and then in 1969–70 to approximately 940,000,000 rupees is an example of this (Chandhok 1990, p. 478). The economic crisis caused primarily by the sudden withdrawal of public investment and a series of crop failures generated the necessary political conditions which led to the Communist parties becoming a part of the government in West Bengal in 1967 (Ray 2011, p. 6).

Amongst other things, the activities of the CPIM would have a decisive role in determining the industrial fate of the province. After the split from the CPI, CPIM would radicalise left politics across India, but particularly in Kerala, Tripura, and West Bengal. In 1970, CPIM would form CITU, its trade union confederation, which would usher in a new wave of trade union militancy across India (Basu 1998, p. ix). The radicalization of the working class that had occurred in the 1960s led to a high tide of industrial action, with strikes and lockouts significantly increasing, both regarding the number of industrial incidents and the number of workers involved (Bhattacherjee 1999, p. 8). 1965 saw 179 strikes and 49 lockouts in West Bengal, and witnessed an increase in labour militancy, as in 1970, there were 678 strikes and 128 lockouts (Roychaudhuri and Basu 2007, p. 12). Labour militancy combined with severe power shortages led to significant capital flight from West Bengal beginning at this time (Bag 2011, pp. 81–2).

The election of the Left Front government in 1977 raised the level of panic among investors to new heights. Following this, a new wave of deindustrialization occurred in West Bengal as industrialists sought to relocate to more capital-friendly parts of India. The 1980s would see the most substantial number of factory closures in India's history (Ramaswamy 2011). During this time, wholly viable and profitable enterprises closed overnight, causing an economic crisis in West Bengal, and a political crisis for the Left Front government. In response to this, the Left Front, through CITU, began to encourage the formation of cooperatives to salvage departing businesses.

The first thing to understand about the strategy of CITU in forming cooperatives is that cooperatives were being formed solely to retain an industrial base in West Bengal. With the CPIM and CITU embracing a productive force determinist reading of Marxism, this necessarily commits them to the idea that it is impossible to change the relations of production and advance even a step toward socialism without the development of productive forces and massive industrialisation. The fact that CPIM were still arguing this point to justify land acquisitions and the creation of special economic zones in the early 2000s is further evidence of this fact. According to their understanding of Marxism, we can safely conclude that CPIM and CITU felt that there was insufficient development in West Bengal to support socialism and were using cooperatives as a strategy to maintain an industrial base, a hypothesis confirmed by the interview data.

The cooperatives formed in West Bengal by CITU, therefore, have a specific character. Defensively formed out of viable enterprises suffering from capital flight, there was no policy by CPIM or CITU to encourage the formation of cooperatives under other circumstances than this. We feel this is a lamentable limitation in the approach taken up by CPIM and CITU; however, it is essential to understand the underlying reasons for their shortsightedness. This decision was not a simple mistake but the result of an underlying ideological approach that limited the possibilities considered by CPIM and CITU, as will be discussed in the next section.

An additional thing to note is CITU's top-down decision to form cooperatives was not a worker-initiated decision. The Alcond Cooperative Management (per Uttam Yadav, director of Alcond) reported that when the cooperatives were set up, it was mostly CITU's doing: "There are many factories here, much labour, the workers of those companies are from CITU and so are we. CITU makes all the foundations you see here. CITU made all the cooperatives and societies; workers did not think of the cooperative ideas, CITU did (Uttam Yadav, 2015, Personal Correspondence)." This particular point emphasises the leading role that workers representatives, whether political parties or trade unions, can play. It is a strong argument against workerism, the idea that the working class will always play the leading role in generating ideas and responses to capital and that they can do so without a revolutionary party organisation. In the case of the Alcond Cooperative, at least initially, CPIM and CITU played a leading role in the Alcond Cooperative's formation and that of many other cooperatives but did not always adequately support these cooperatives. Therefore, the

Alcond Cooperative provides a critical case study of cooperative operations under the umbrella of the ruling party of a provincial government.

In addition to understanding West Bengal's economic history, it is also essential to understand the economic conditions that have surrounded Alcond's demise. Looking at the current economic situation allows us to explore the question of whether cooperatives and the drive of workers, trade unions and political organisations to form them, is vulnerable to liberalisation. Alternatively, is it the subjective factors, the ideology of individual political actors that can be held to explain the decline of Alcond and other cooperatives.

After India's liberalisation in 1994, the post-liberalization period did not change very much regarding the deindustrialization of West Bengal. Despite the Left Front government's active connivance with the liberalisation agenda, courting private investors and utilising state power invite private capital to industrialise the state, capital continued to drain from West Bengal leading to some industries and industrial units in bad shape. In 2005, a report was published by Nagarik Mancha demonstrated the extent of the ill health of the industry in West Bengal, which provided case studies of fourteen different major industrial units that closed (Nagarik Manch 2005).

A significant question that raised here is why in the 1980s when capital and industries were draining from West Bengal, were the workers able to force state intervention and the facilitation of cooperative formation. By comparison, why is such a movement absent if the state faces a similar industrial decline such as can be seen in the 2000s.

In the 1980s, we have seen that CITU led the drive for the formation of cooperatives as a means of responding to the plight facing its members and also the Left Front government. Capital is still draining from West Bengal, with several high profile examples such as the closure of the Dunlop Rubber Factory in Hooghly impacting scores of workers (Sen and Dasgupta 2009, p. 116). Additionally, there is a well-established link between deindustrialization that has occurred and the progressive weakening of trade union power in West Bengal (with CITU the largest trade union and therefore the worst impacted) (Basu 2014). It is therefore interesting to note that CITU's support of cooperative formation appears to have dropped off. However, this is not to say that there is no longer pressure from works and other organisations to form cooperatives.

In 1999, in West Bengal itself, there was a plan made by the employees of the Bengal Ingot company to run their unit as a cooperative (Mukherjee 1999). Similarly, there is the story of Kamani Tubes Limited, which was taken over by a workers' cooperative in 1988 in a move sanctioned by the Board of Industrial and Financial Reconstruction (Kamani Tubes 2015). Kamani was a unique case, as the workers petitioned the Supreme Court of India to use the capital from their provident funds to take over the business (Vanniarajan 1999, pp. 362–3). The cooperative struggled to maintain itself before being revived after a lengthy legal battle by the social entrepreneur, Kalpana Saroj, in 2011 (Karunakaran 2011). Notably, even the right-wing Rashtriya Swayamsevak Sangh-affiliated Bharatiya Mazdoor Sangh (Indian Workers Union, BMS henceforth) publicly advocates for cooperative formation. They call this "labourisation," using the example of the New Central Jute Mill, which they claim as a successful example of a cooperative formation that was pursued despite the opposition of the central government and the Left Front government in West Bengal (Vanniarajan 1999, p. 364). There will be further discussion of the ideological approach to the cooperative formation of BMS and other unions later in this chapter.

In the 1980s, there seemed to be a healthy workers' movement in West Bengal advocating for the formation of cooperatives. This movement was linked closely with CITU and indirectly with the Left Front government as part of the wave of mass mobilisation that brought the Left Front to power. With a similar wave of company closures occurring in the late 1990s up until now, it is worth noting that there is still evidence of worker enthusiasm for cooperative formation. What has changed appears to be the willingness of CITU and CPIM to encourage cooperative formation in their political work.

As part of our interviews, we met with Kanak Bhaduri, CITU's Convenor of Cooperatives. His job was to help organise the existing cooperatives, to establish new ones, and to educate cooperative members on the principles of cooperatives. Bhaduri's assessment of the decline of the CITU cooperative movement is revealing about the attitudinal shift and emphasis in CITU. When we asked why CITU workers seemed to no longer be forming cooperatives, he replied that "Actually it is up to them, depending on the consciousness of the workers. If they have a desire to run a cooperative like this, then they can get support." We can see however that the desire to form cooperatives remains both in West Bengal and in India more generally, and the objective conditions are very similar to those in the 1980s. The subjective response from CPIM and CITU has changed owing to a decline in the radicalism of the CPIM and CITU's political orientation over time.

Ideology and Cooperative Formation

In this section, we will discuss the relationship between political ideologies and the approach taken by political organisations, social organisations, and trade unions toward cooperative formation. This will involve a survey of the approaches to cooperatives taken by the Indian labour movement. We will focus on CPIM and CITU given that the focus of this chapter is the Alcond Cooperative, but consider the other main trade unions also. We conclude the chapter with a comparison between the relatively defensive approach of the Indian trade unions that have formed cooperatives to save dying enterprises, and the proactive approach of the Mondragon cooperatives in the Basque region.

To fully understand the formation and operation of the Alcond Cooperative, it is necessary to have an understanding of the CPIM and its trade union organisation, CITU, as these are the parent organisations of the Alcond Cooperative. In this section, we will specifically address the ideological position of CPIM, their understanding of socialism, and their approach to cooperative building formation. It is notable that across the broad Indian left, no left political forces have actively promoted cooperative formation as a crucial part of their political strategy. Defensive use of cooperatives is the norm in India, and this perspective is something we are hoping to change. In this section, we will demonstrate the way that cooperatives were set up, not as an alternative model of production, but only as a way to retain jobs and industry in the state of West Bengal.

The CPIM embrace a productive force determinist reading of Marxism, important in understanding their approach to cooperatives. A reading of Marxism based on productive force determinism stresses the historical role of productive forces and their ability to determine the relations of production and therefore the mode of production. This understanding of Marxism is the "orthodox" understanding of Marxist at the time as it was the Marxism espoused in the Soviet Union, and by the original Communist Party of India (CPI henceforth) before its division. We can see this philosophy through an examination of the discourse of key CPIM leaders.

Consider, for example, Sitaram Yechury, the current General Secretary of the CPIM, who said (Yechury 1999),

> *It would be erroneous to conclude that under socialism the market will cease to exist. So long as commodities are produced, the market exists. The crucial question is not planning versus market but which dominates what. Under social-*

ism, the market is one of the means for the distribution of the social product. Centralised planning, utilising the market forces and the market indicators, will be able to efficiently develop the productive forces and meet the welfare demands of the people. Therefore, ignoring market indicators leads to greater irrational use of resources, which will adversely affect the plan process itself.

Alternatively, consider former General Secretary Prakash Karat (Karat 2000), who said.

The task of the agrarian revolution is directed against the elimination of this form of landlordism and the survivals of semi-feudal relations so that the existing relations of production can be transformed and the way opened for the rapid development of the productive forces.

The key to this analysis is the comment that only by developing the productive forces can the needs of the people be met. In other words, Yechury and Karat both argue that changes to the relations of production alone cannot satisfy the needs of the citizens. This interpretation of Marxism is critical to understanding CPIM and the way they understood the role of cooperatives in West Bengal. CPIM cooperatives have tended to focus on the retention of industry and a development of productive capacity, rather than a change in relations of production, despite the emphasis that workers in cooperative enterprises emphasize the latter.

CPIM imagined an India that was significantly underdeveloped for the transition to capitalism, let alone socialism. In their view, India needed to accomplish the task of the "people's democratic revolution," a fundamental concept in CPIM ideology. Karat, quoting the CPIM party program initially outlined in 1964, describes the people's democratic revolution in the following terms (Karat 2000):

Unlike in the advanced capitalist countries where capitalism grew on the ashes of pre-capitalist society, which was destroyed by the rising bourgeoisie, capitalism in India was super-imposed on pre-capitalist society. Neither the British colonialists during their rule nor the Indian bourgeoisie assuming power after independence attempted to smash it, which was one of the most important preconditions for the free development of capitalism. The present Indian society, therefore, is a peculiar combination of monopoly capitalist domination with caste, communal and tribal institutions. It has thus fallen on the working class and its party to unite all the progressive forces interested in destroying the precapitalist society and to consolidate the revolutionary forces within it so as to facilitate the completion of the democratic revolution and prepare the ground for the transition to socialism.

Writing in the year 2000, Karat confirmed that the CPIM still felt they had not yet achieved the task of the people's democratic revolution, a position that CPIM holds to this day. What we can conclude from this is that throughout the history of The Alcond Cooperative's existence, and throughout the entire Left Front government, CPIM held the position that they were assisting the development of capitalism to "prepare the grounds for socialism." The argument follows that there would need to be a sustained period of capitalist development, corresponding with the destruction of the pre-capitalist society. During this time, the party would work to ameliorate the effects of capitalism on the working class and peasantry of India (Surjeet 2000). In the end, however, the productive forces and their development would decide when India would reach socialism.

A split in the CPI led to the formation of CPIM, generated by the nexus between the Soviet Union and the Indian National Congress, India's most successful political party in the post-independence period. The Soviet assessment was that the Congress Party represented a progressive class agenda, that of India's national bourgeoisie. Additionally, the Soviet position suggested that State Capitalism was a progressive social form above other forms of capitalism, particularly in newly independent countries. Anastas Mikoyan, the Soviet First Deputy Chairman for the Council of Ministers, in the 8th Congress of the Chinese Communist Party, commented that "we must be able to see the differences between state capitalism in India and capitalism in the United States" and further that "Marxists cannot but regard positively…[this] new transitional form to avoid capitalism" (Rey 1986, p. 33).

As such, the Soviets felt that the Congress Party could complete the task of nation-building to prepare the material ground for socialism. Already in this book, we have touched on the Bhilai Steel Plant in Chhattisgarh as being an example of the aggressive promotion of capital-intensive heavy industry and formalised employment as a result of Soviet industrial development policy in India. The underlying understanding here is the requirement for significant material development in India to change the relations of production and facilitate socialism eventually.

As a result of this partnership, the Soviet Union attempted to moderate the actions of the CPI against the Indian state, which led to serious internal divisions within the party and its eventual split. The activists who would eventually split and form the CPIM would argue that the Indian National Congress represented the interests of land-owning feudal elements and therefore were unlikely to complete the task of the new democratic revolution and the establishment of democratic capitalism.

The CPIM emerged as an independent political force that was prepared to contest the Congress party. CPIM changed Indian politics in the various areas where they obtained higher levels of influence, such as West Bengal, Kerala, and Tripura. While the CPIM had split with the CPI over the question of the class character of the Indian National Congress and the role of the Soviet Union, its politics retained some Khrushchevite policy positions. The most notable of these was the commitment to a peaceful transformation from capitalism to socialism advocated by the Soviet Union in its 20th Congress. This philosophical position led the CPIM to renounce revolutionary struggle in favour of electoral politics.

The coming to power of the CPIM in West Bengal in 1977 represented a critical moment for the working class history in India, and a test case for the ability of electoral politics to deliver the outcomes desired by Marxists. For the first time, there was a democratically elected, communist party in power in one of India's provinces. This political context would be the backdrop for the emergence of some cooperatives, and among them, the Alcond factory.

In comparing the approach of CPIM and CITU to cooperative formation, with the other mainstream political forces in India, a notable feature is that their strategy centres on defensive cooperative formation. When an enterprise is mismanaged or failing, there is a significant impetus for the company to be taken over by its workers. However, there appears to be a lack of a proactive, cooperative strategy, with most unions in India not aiming to form cooperatives to improve the institutional power of the working class but rather to retain employment or an industrial base.

There are alternative ideological reasons why some other trade union movements in India have eschewed cooperative formation as a strategy. In the case of the BMS, the BMS pays lip service to the idea of "labourisation," which they see as a form of cooperative formation. In truth, however, labourisation is based on a methodological individualist approach where individual workers are converted into shareholders of their firms through employee stock ownership plans (Vanniarajan 1999 p. 366). The BMS has also used their argument for cooperative formation as a way of supporting government attempts to privatise firms based on the idea that individual workers can then become shareholders in the privatised firms (ibid.). The majority of the justification provided by BMS in favour of cooperative formation is that it improves the productivity of industrial units by harmonising work relations and giving significant incentives to workers to improve productivity (ibid, pp. 365–6).

Vannirajan (1999, p. 365) stated that the Communist Party of India-affiliated All India Trade Union Congress has historically argued against cooperative formation, suggesting that "AITUC is of the opinion that labourisation does not give any additional right to workers in the management of industry." While it is hard to find primary source materials from AITUC or CPI to corroborate this position, one historical example does lend support to Vannirajan's ideas. In West Bengal itself, the Sonali Tea Estate was taken over by the Cha Bagan Workers Union, affiliated to AITUC (Ness and Azzelini 2011, p. 362). The reaction of the CPI to this takeover was to expel the union's general secretary from the union and the CPI, after which it has been argued that CPI and AITUC did not support cooperative formation (ibid.). Despite this, the CPI has been supportive of some forms of worker ownership where workers become shareholders in privatised firms (Candland 2001, p. 90). In this sense, their position is remarkably similar to that of the BMS.

While Vannirajan is a public advocate for the merits of BMS, it should be noted that other unions participated in the New Central Jute Mills cooperative movement, with 12 unions involved in total (Vannirajan 1999, p. 364). This includes the Congress Party-affiliated Indian Trade Union Congress (INTUC), whom we have not yet discussed. INTUC's participation in the New Central Jute Mills venture indicates that INTUC is broadly supportive of the idea of worker-shareholding ownership, and one of INTUC's leaders, Subrata Mukherjee, is on the NCJM board of directors (ibid, p. 365).

From this, we can see that across the Indian trade union movement, there is a reasonable convergence around the idea of workers as shareholders in businesses. This is qualified by the fact that unions tend to be supportive of the idea of workers as shareholders only in protective cases, where businesses are withdrawing investment, or when the government is privatising its concerns, and the workers feel they can continue to run the enterprise in a viable way. There is less broad support within the union movement for cooperative formation where the enterprises are owned collectively rather than on a shareholder basis, such as in the Alcond Cooperative. Again, in these cases, the cooperatives have been formed defensively in response to declining industry as opposed to proactively.

The defensive approach to cooperatives compares poorly to a more proactive approach. To demonstrate this, we will briefly highlight the approach of the Mondragon Cooperatives of the Basque region. We feel this is an appropriate comparison to make, given that there is a significant industrial focus in the Mondragon cooperatives, making it comparable to CITU's efforts to form industrial cooperatives and those of the Indian trade union movement in general. Secondly, the fact that Mondragon's history begins during the fascist regime of General Fransisco Franco demonstrates the possibilities of organising under the most difficult of circumstances. The Mondragon cooperatives are perhaps the most successful worker-run organisations in current existence. While this is not the appropriate book to discuss the Mondragon cooperatives in detail, we will present a comparison regarding the ideology of cooperative promotion, and the proactive strategy.

As has been noted in this chapter, the majority of industrial cooperatives in India have been formed defensively, and most trade unions have an ideological approach that is supportive of cooperative formation under limited circumstances. In the Mondragon case, it is notable that several years of preparation went into the development of the cooperative movement, with a clear objective of cooperative formation forming part of the explicit goals of the movement.

The Mondragon story begins with the arrival of a Basque Catholic priest, Jose Maria Arizmendiarrieta (Arizmendi hereafter), who had served in the Basque army during the Spanish Civil War and narrowly escaped execution. After being sent to Mondragon in 1941, Arizmendi spent significant effort in developing the social base that would eventually transform into the world's most substantial cooperative movement. He would do so by reviving church organisations for working-class youth and families and using this organisational strength to build institutions such as a medical clinic, a school, and a technical college (Whyte and Whyte 1991, p. 29).

Arizmendi used these institutions as a platform to spread an ideology of "cooperation and collective solidarity" and the idea that work should have dignity, ideas that find their origins in Catholic social thought (ibid). He also promoted grassroots democracy, where members of the organisations would vote on who would manage them. This grassroots democracy then transitioned into workplace democracy when the industrial cooperatives would be formed. Arizmendi utilised his network of institutions to raise money for what would become the first workers' cooperative industry in Mondragon, a domestic appliance company that would eventually become Fagor Electrodomesticos. The success of this corporation coupled with the ideology supporting cooperatives led to the proactive expansion of the cooperative movement in Mondragon with an active attempt to cooperativize the entire economy of the town. While Fagor Electrodomesticos closed as a result of the Spanish debt crisis, Mondragon Corporation remains an ongoing success story, employing 74,117 people and generating revenue of 11.8 billion Euros (Mondragon Corporation 2014).

The Mondragon cooperatives demonstrate the possibilities associated with a proactive approach to cooperative formation, coupled with an ideology that values the development of cooperatives. The difference between this approach and the approach of the major trade unions in India is stark. We feel that the lack of a proactive approach to cooperative building is one of the critical factors that limited the potential of the Alcond Cooperative and the other industrial cooperatives of West Bengal and India. This is a significant factor behind Alcond's current crisis.

The Alcond Wire Factory: History, Processes, and Problems

In this section, we will document the history of the Alcond Cooperative, as well as the technical and organisational aspects of the factory. We will conclude with a discussion of some of the recent problems the Alcond Cooperative has been facing. The overall experience of the Alcond Cooperative will allow us to summarise the key lessons that the Alcond Cooperative experience can teach other activists and the social movements interested in cooperative formation.

The Alcond factory in its privately owned version was initially opened in 1959 as Alcond Aluminium UP Private Ltd. but closed in 1982 when the original owners of the factory withdrew their investment. At this point, a protracted struggle would develop around who would control the factory site. Alcond's workers were keen to continue factory operations and to run the factory as a cooperative but faced certain legal hurdles such as obtaining legal title to the property and machinery of the factory. With the assistance of the Left Front government, who purchased the property, the Alcond Cooperative was eventually able to gain control of the factory and open its doors on 6 April 1989 with 230 workers. The method of property transfer was an essential aspect of the formation of the cooperative. While the actual business license belonged to the workers cooperative, the land itself became the property of a department of the West Bengal government. This was significant in the short-term, as it means the workers had few assets to leverage against possible bank loans, but it was also significant in the long term, as it established a form of structural dependency on the West Bengal state government.

From the outset, the very nature of production in the Alcond factory created certain conditions that governed the formation of the cooperative. To better understand this, it is first necessary to describe the technical nature of their production. The Alcond factory's primary purpose as an industrial unit is to create various kinds of conductors and wire for power transmission. The factory begins the manufacturing process with aluminium strips and conducts the necessary cutting and spooling necessary to build large drums of electrical wire that are then used to conduct electricity from power stations and sub-stations all over India.

While the Alcond Cooperative existed in the informal sector, it is notable that the Alcond Cooperative is an example of capital-intensive production. As such, to turn the enterprise into a cooperative, a significant amount of money was required. Firstly, it was necessary to purchase the enterprise and its productive assets, including various pieces of heavy machinery. Secondly, Alcond needed a sum of working capital to conduct the day-to-day business of the company. The necessary funds for both the acquisition of the company and the working capital would need to be sought by a bank loan.

Initially, government banks were reluctant to loan to a cooperatively owned and run enterprises like the Alcond Cooperative, particularly when there was little the workers could offer regarding security against the loan. It was not until the Left Front government used its political power by acting as guarantor of a loan and using government money to put up a deposit that Alcond was able to secure the necessary working capital and commence production. The Left Front government also invested 7,000,000 rupees (in 1989 value) for raw materials, machinery, and general factory modernization.

The Left Front government guaranteed 20% of government tenders to cooperative societies. This created a stable revenue stream for the cooperative, while also allowing the cooperative to provide a service to the West Bengal government in its attempts to resolve notorious power problems and electrify the province. While a significant portion of the Alcond Cooperative's business came through this symbiotic link with the Left Front, it is notable that the Alcond Cooperative supplied materials all over India. For example, Alcond's records indicated that their turnover in the province of Maharashtra amounted to over 70,000,000 rupees in total value.

After this investment, the Alcond Cooperative ran as a viable enterprise. It gradually expanded its business and the number of workers it was able to employ. From an initial 240 workers, it grew to a high of 600 employees in the early 1990s. This was the cooperative's golden age. The Alcond

Cooperative would be stricken by India's adoption of neoliberal economic reform in 1994, but at the same time, it would also demonstrate the ability of worker cooperatives to resist neoliberalism. In 1995, the central government stopped providing subsidies for electricity to the various provincial governments. As the Alcond Cooperative's primary client base involved provincial government electricity corporations, this generated its first major crisis as it suffered a significant loss of business, simultaneous increase in expenditure, and a new wave of capital flight from West Bengal.

A critical moment in the financial history of the Alcond Cooperative was when they delivered a significant supply of goods to the West Bengal Electricity Board in 1995. After receiving the goods, the Board did not pay for them, causing a massive cash flow problem for the cooperative. It would be five years until the board would settle half of its debts as a result of political pressure from the Left Front government. Half of this debt remains unpaid to this day.

The Left Front government intervened to support the Alcond Cooperative by providing a non-refundable state grant of 20,000,000 rupees. The role of the Left Front government is again seen to be a critical feature of the success of the Alcond Cooperative in difficult surrounding circumstances. The Alcond Cooperative's managing director had the following to say about the Left Front:

> *When the Left Front government was there, the system worked so well, because every time there was a difficulty we would get support. In 1996 the layout of the factory was increased. In 1995 the funding from Delhi stopped for electricity. After 1995-6, when the funding stopped, capital was draining from West Bengal, and the problem with the electricity board started. From 1996-9 the workers would come and go because we could not guarantee to pay their salaries consistently. Our balance went to zero. We still fought, and the Left Front government gave a two crore grant (Bipul Bhattacharjee, Personal Correspondence, 2015).*

With the election of the Bharatiya Janata Party-led National Democratic Alliance as India's central government in 1998, there would be an acceleration of neoliberal reforms. Many of these reforms would impact the Alcond Cooperative's work. For example, in 2004, the government's policy of privatising non-profitable assets led to the privatisation of government-owned electricity boards such as BNSL and the West Bengal board. This would dramatically alter the terms of the relationship between the Alcond Cooperative and its most significant customers.

In addition to the production-related aspects, the Alcond Cooperative employees have regular political meetings as well. In these meetings, there are discussions about political events and objectives and Marxist theory. CITU also organises regular programs where union and political education occurs, and where cooperative members can share their experiences with union members who work with private companies. Despite being a trade union-run concern, the Alcond Cooperative employees regularly participate in strikes called by India's various central trade unions (of which CITU is one). In this regard, the Alcond Cooperative is unlike the other cooperatives studied in this project. Neither the Chhattisgarh Mines Shramik Sangh, the Chhattisgarh Mukti Morcha cooperatives nor the Self-Employed Women's Association devoted any attention to the political education of its members at the time we conducted our fieldwork.

As far as the working conditions are concerned, first, each member of the cooperative was considered a 'shareholder' in the cooperative and possessed shares of about 7500 rupees in current prices (approximately $125). Historically, the members of the cooperatives did not attempt to reclaim their shares even on retirement, although this was changed forcibly in 2012 due to intervention from the Trinamool Congress Government. In this way, we can see the ideological changes being forced by the new government on the cooperative ethos built by the movement.

We were fortunate to interview some of the original members of the cooperative who had also worked for the Alcond factory when it was privately run. The workers reported that it was a "hell and heaven" difference when the factory became cooperatively owned. Workers were consulted as part of the decision-making process, and the status of the workers changed. Notably, however, the workers reported a significant improvement regarding their pay and conditions. With the workers effectively gaining control of their means of production, they reported a significant improvement in the productivity of the factory. As a result of this, the Alcond Cooperative was able to pay production bonuses whenever a significant contract was completed.

In addition to the material benefits of cooperative formation, psychological benefits were reported by the workers. Some examples can be given of this. Firstly, the workers spoke with pride about their ability to manage and run a complex enterprise for so long. In particular, they highlighted the fact that each worker, despite his/her specialisation, knew how to perform every task at the factory "from sweeper to manager." The workers noted that they had developed a meaningful sense of self-reliance regarding the production operations of the factory, with the workers themselves designing and building many complex machines and machine tools to avoid the need for them to be ordered or imported. A particular moment of happiness for the Alcond Cooperative workers was when they were able to show us the single piece of imported machinery in the factory, which was a colossal implement imported from Germany in the 1990s. The Alcond Cooperative workers' machines stood proudly side by side with this piece of high technology equipment as a testament to the creative and technical potential of working-class people.

The sense of dedication to the enterprise was evident in that despite the current financial struggles, so many of the Alcond Cooperative's workers continued to work in the factory, even contributing work on an effectively voluntary basis as the cooperative was not in a position to pay their full wages. A similar story can be told about workers who had retired upon reaching retirement age. Many of these workers continued coming back after retirement and receiving only casual rates of pay; such was the attachment that they felt to their enterprise. The Alcond Cooperative's management reported that often they would contradict CITU's policy on engaging casual workers to retain retired workers, both for sentimental reasons but also for the immense technical skills and experience that the workers brought to the enterprise and its younger workers.

Lessons of the Alcond Cooperative

At the time of writing this book, the Alcond Cooperative, a once proud and viable enterprise, is but a shell of its original existence. This factory, which survived India's neoliberal turn with reasonably limited support even from "friendly" forces such as the Left Front government, appears locked into a slow demise due to a lack of working capital. There are, however, some meaningful conclusions that can be drawn from its experience.

Firstly, the Alcond Cooperative demonstrated the ability of workers and trade unions to self-manage a technically complex and capital-intensive production process. Whether or not the CPIM felt the relations of production could change under capitalism, the cooperative's workers offered yet more evidence that changes in the relations of production are possible without the development of the productive forces. To this end, we can see that CPIM grossly underestimated the power of the working class in West Bengal and the importance of courting private capital. The Alcond Cooperative provides evidence that it is possible to industrialise and run industrial concerns without depending on the capitalist market.

Secondly, the Alcond Cooperative demonstrated the critical role that state support can play in the formation of cooperatives. The Left Front government in West Bengal were hardly enthusiastic supporters of the cooperatives. However, the limited support that was given, such as the guaranteeing of loans, was instrumental to their survival, as were the regular orders for production from the state.

The other side of this state dependence, however, is that as soon as the Left Front was not there to support the Alcond Cooperative, severe difficulties were faced that contributed to its current crisis. The limitations of basing a political strategy around holding a provincial government in India are therefore made apparent by this case. Alcond, therefore, adds to a growing list of reasons to be sceptical about Khrushchevite political strategies such as those pursued by CPIM based on electoral success, and the role of provincial government politics in India.

We would argue that the Alcond Cooperative succeeded for a significant period, against all the odds. To paraphrase the late Ernesto "Che" Guevara, we believe that cooperative's example demonstrates the need to create two or three many different Alconds. If a cooperative like this can be successful with limited support and without a real strategy for cooperative enterprises to take over the economic base, then we can only wonder how successful it can be with proper strategy and active support.

This was the big takeaway lesson from the Alcond example, particularly when compared with the Mondragon cooperatives in Spain. Mondragon has been successful because of a variety of factors: an ideology supporting collectivism and cooperative formation, the building of a broad social base of institutional support and a proactive strategy towards forming cooperatives and extending them to change the power relations in society. By contrast, most industrial cooperatives in India, including Alcond, have formed defensively, attempted to revive only dying industries, lacked a social base of support, and not tried to extend their influence beyond the individual industrial unit. The success of Mondragon against the isolation of Alcond and the other cooperatives in West Bengal and elsewhere highlight the importance of this comparison.

References

Bag, K. 2011. Red Bengal's rise and fall. *New Left Review*, vol. 70.

Basu, J. 1998. Introductory Note. *Documents of the Communist Party of India, vol XIV,* National Book Agency Private Limited: Kolkata.

Basu, M. 2014, *Study looks into why West Bengal's trade unions are now weaker*, Available from: http://www.livemint.com/Industry/PmEwcYGGH1SadedoKgZ9cK/Study-looks-into-why-West-Bengals-trade-unions-are-now-weak.html.

Bhattacherjee, D. 1999, *Organized labor and economic liberalization India: Past and present*. International Institute for Labour Studies, Geneva.

Candland, C. 2001. The cost of incorporation: Labor institutions, industrial restructuring, and new trade union strategies in India and Pakistan. The politics of labor in a global age: Continuity and change in late-industrializing and post-socialist economies.

Chandhok, HL. 1990. *India database: Volume 1*. Living Media India, New Delhi.

International Cooperative Alliance. 2012. *Mamata pushes cooperatives on suicidal course*. Available from: http://ica.coop/en/media/thenews/mamata-pushes-cooperatives-suicidal-course.

Kamani Tubes. 2015. *Kamani Tubes*. Available from: http://kamanitubes.com/.

Karat, P. 2000, CPI(M) Programme: Basic strategy reiterated. *The Marxist*. Vol. 16, no. 3. Available from: http://www.cpim.org/marxist/200003_marxist_progrm_pk.htm.

Karunakaran, N. 2011. *How Dalit entrepreneur Kalpana Saroj revived Kamani Tubes Ltd*. Available from: http://articles.economictimes.indiatimes.com/2011-07-29/news/29829281_1_dalit-kamani-tubes-ktl.

Lahiri, A & Yi, K. 2004. *A tale of two states*. Available from: http://core.ac.uk/download/pdf/6366629.pdf.

Mondragon Corporation. 2014. *Annual Report*. Available from: http://www.mondragon-corporation.com/eng/about-us/economic-and-financial-indicators/annual-report/

Mukherjee, A. 1999. *Bengal Ingot employees to run unit, submits revival plan*. Available from: http://expressindia.indianexpress.com/fe/daily/19990624/fco24003.html

Nagarik Manch. 2005. *Factory closures and plight of workers: A comprehensive summary of Bengal's industrial condition*. Available from: http://sanhati.com/excerpted/1233/.

Ness, I. and Azzellini, D. 2011. *Ours to Master and to Own: Workers' Control from the Commune to the Present*. Chicago: Haymarket Books.

Patnaik, Prabhat. 2006. Three Decades of Left Front Rule in Bengal. *Nature, Society and Thought*. Vol 19, Iss 4.

Patnaik, Prabhat. 2011. *The Myths of Capitalism*. Available from: https://mronline.org/2011/07/04/the-myths-of-capitalism/

Ramaswamy, V. 2011, "It does not die" – Urban protest in Kolkata, 1987–2007. *Samaj: South Asia Multidisciplinary Academic Journal*. Vol. 5.

Ray, S. 2011. The political economy of decline of industry in West Bengal: Experiences of a Marxist state within a mixed economy. Available from: http://web2.uconn.edu/economics/working/2011-10.pdf.

Rey, H. 1986. *Sino-Soviet conflict over India: An analysis of the causes of conflict between Moscow and Beijing over India since 1949*. Abhinav Publications: Delhi.

Roychaudhuri, Ajitabha and Basu, Gautam Kumar. 2007. The Decline and Recent Resurgence of the Manufacturing sector of West Bengal: Implications for Pro-Poor Growth from and Institutional Point of View. IPPG Discussion Paper No 10, University of Manchester, UK.

Sen, S & Dasgupta, B. 2009. *Unfreedom and Waged Work: Labour in India's Manufacturing Industry.* Sage India, New Delhi.

Surjeet, HS. 2000, Programme updated with changing times. *The Marxist*, Vol. 16, No 3. Available from: http://cpim.org/content/programme-updated-changing-times

The Telegraph. 2013. *HC strikes down cooperative act.* Available from: http://www.telegraphindia.com/1130914/jsp/bengal/story_17348497.jsp#.Ve1CeRGqpBc

Vanniarajan, R. 1999. Labourisation in India. *Indian Journal of Industrial Relations.* Vol 34, Iss 3: 361–367.

Whyte, WF & Whyte, KK. 1991. *Making Mondragon: The growth and dynamics of the worker cooperative complex.* Cornell University Press: London.

Yechury, S. 1999. The road to socialism in China. *The Marxist.* Vol. 15, No. 4. Available from: http://www.cpim.org/marxist/199904_marxist_china_sry.htm.

CHAPTER 5

Trade Union Imperialism and a Non-transformative Approach: SEWA Rachaita

The Self-Employed Women's Association is almost universally praised for its work in organising women in India's informal sector but has never been examined from a critical perspective. In this study, we critically assess the SEWA movement both regarding its big-picture strategy, and the grassroots of its movement. We find that the strategies and tactics employed by SEWA expose the Indian working class to significant imperialist intervention through donations by highly politicised groups which have given these groups significant leverage over the organisation.

An essential subject discussed in this chapter is the extent to which the activities of SEWA have improved or restricted the agency of working-class women. This will be assessed both generally regarding their overall organisation, but also in a specific case of their construction workers' cooperative movement situated in Ahmedabad, Gujarat, India. An important debate which has been discussed primarily within the disciplines of human and labour geography concerns workers' agency within specific spaces (Herod 1997, 1998, 2001; Wills 1998, Coe and Jordhus-Lier 2010). Coe and Jordhus-Lier have further argued that "agency is relational and can only ever

This chapter is an extended version of article titled 'Labour imperialism in India: The case of SEWA' authored by Timothy Kerswell and Surendra Pratap, published in Geoforum, Elsevier.

T. Kerswell, S. Pratap, *Worker Cooperatives in India*,
https://doi.org/10.1007/978-981-13-0384-5_5

be understood as such by considering, in turn, labour's positionality concerning global production networks, the state and the public sector, the wider community and labour market intermediaries (Ibid, p. 214)".

Unions, as representatives of workers, act as principal labour market intermediaries and in many cases play essential roles in the community and even in government. This chapter endeavours to contribute to the understanding of how SEWA and its approach to both trade unionism and cooperatives in India but also in the global South more generally. In turn, we also hope to demonstrate the hegemonization of SEWA by trade union imperialism, which in combination with the location of informal sector workers within global production networks, contributes significantly to their disempowerment. We also note that SEWA is characterised by an ideology of liberal entrepreneurialism which enables the movement to seamlessly dovetail with imperialist organisations, and with an overall narrative that is supportive of neoliberal capitalism, albeit with a human face.

On the micro-level, our study is based on in-depth interviews with SEWA leaders and construction cooperative members undertaken in the summer of 2015. We will demonstrate that far from significantly improving the welfare of Indian working class women, SEWA's Rachaita Construction Cooperative leverages the social prestige of the SEWA organisation, including amongst its members, to deliver pay and conditions which are poor even by capitalistic labour market standards. SEWA institutions contribute to a deradicalization of the Indian working class, as well as a deradicalization of Indian working women about gender politics.

Writers such as Agarwala (2013), have argued that organisations like SEWA constitute a new form of politics, namely the politics of the Indian informal sector, which they consider the only acceptable method to follow under globalisation. We believe that such perspectives should be left apologists for globalisation. Against this, we hope to demonstrate that SEWA, rather than help Indian working class women, is instead damaging their long-term prospects for advancement through a maintenance of informality and the deleterious conditions associated with it, and a steady process of disempowerment.

We will argue that SEWA as an organisation is a product of hegemonic forms of imperialism, both in the trade union imperialism discussed by Scipes (2010a) as well as hegemonic imperialism from the US government itself. SEWA's rise to significance can be seen in the spread of SEWA to various parts of India, but also importantly, to different countries in the global South and on the international stage in the UN apparatus and the international trade union movement (Kerswell and Pratap 2017).

Accounts of SEWA

To date, accounts of SEWA have been overwhelmingly positive, and our work stands in dialogue with these accounts providing a critical counter-narrative where one does not presently exist. The landmark study/history of SEWA is *Where Women are Leaders* by Kalima Rose. Rose is notable for her connection to the Women's World Banking organisation, and later in this chapter, we will discuss the crucial interlinkages between SEWA and various international donors, as well as the impact these donations have on the SEWA project and its ideology. As can be seen from the title, Rose presents an extremely positive account of SEWA. Following on from the work of Rose, SEWA has been treated under the broad rubric of empowerment (Datta 2003, p. 351).

Most recently, Agarwala (2013) has made a series of arguments in her book *Informal Labor, Formal Politics and Dignified Discontent in India,* which by her admission is significantly influenced by SEWA ideology (p. xv). At the core of these claims is the idea that informal sector workers constitute a new class identity and wage a new class struggle which focuses on empowerment and the extraction of gains from the state, rather than from the capitalist class.

Regarding critical perspectives on SEWA, there is very little which has been said in either academic or activist literature. Hensman (2011) discusses various strategies and tactics of SEWA mostly positively throughout her book. However, buried in an endnote, there is an anecdotal story of a SEWA cleaner she met who complained about low wages, which upon investigation led her to discover that rival unions reported SEWA members defecting to them to achieve higher wages. In the entirety of the literature on SEWA, this endnote is the extent of criticism. In this respect, we hope to provide a much-needed supplement regarding critical perspectives on SEWA.

The chapter begins by reviewing various praising perspectives of SEWA from different perspectives. We follow this up by highlighting some causes for skepticism rooted in SEWA's strategy, tactics and international partnerships. Following this, we will analyse SEWA's ideology which we see as the critical link between their behaviour as an organisation, and the structuring of the cooperative that forms part of our case study. Finally, we will examine the methods used in the SEWA Rachaita construction cooperative documenting the structure of the organisation, the working conditions and other essential features assessing whether SEWA has contributed to the welfare of working-class women in the construction sector.

Reasons for Skepticism

Scholarship on SEWA has tended to present it as a successful model of informal sector organising and has been overwhelmingly positive to date. In response to this, we wish to highlight several less discussed features of SEWA as an organisation as we believe this integrates well with the empirical work we conducted during our field visits. It is not our intention to dismiss the positive work which SEWA does. During our field research, we met several dedicated and committed activists and workers whose struggle should be appreciated. Instead we intend to highlight specific ideological weaknesses and their sources in SEWA practice. We will begin with the global before turning to the local examples which we documented.

The literature on imperialism, and specifically labour imperialism, is extremely helpful to analyse the role of US labour in the deradicalization of working-class movements in the third world. There was a wave of scholarship from the late 1960s to the 1970s which studied the negative impact of US trade unionism on labour movements in the third world. Radosh (1969) argued that US Labor did the bidding of the US government in the international arena. Thomson and Larson (1978) and Scott (1978) conducted studies focused primarily on the role of US labor imperialism in Latin America, particularly in the fallout of the coup against the Allende government in Chile. Schmidt (1978) discussed the role of the American Federation of Teachers in international affairs in partnership with the CIA.

Following this, there was another wave of scholarship in the late 1980s which considered the role of US labour in Nicaragua, Guatemala and El Salvador (Scipes 2010a, p. xxii). Scipes (Ibid) notes that the key approach of critical labour foreign policy studies from Radosh in the late 1960s until the end of the 1980s was an approach that saw US labour as pawns of the US government, a kind of 'external control' theory.

From the perspective of labour geography, the leading scholar to consider the relationship between labour imperialism and labour geography is Glassman (2004) who argued that the breakdown in the accord between labour and capital in the United States has not weakened the imperialistic tendencies of US unions in their international policy.

Southall (1995, p. 45) advanced the theory of trade union imperialism by demonstrating that rather than being taken over by the US government or the CIA, the dynamics of trade union imperialism come internally from the US labour movement itself. Drawing this analysis together is Scipes (2010a, b), whose work represents the most detailed account of labour imperialism to date. Scipes (2010a, p. xxvii) presents a 'hegemonic' perspective of trade union imperialism, whereby US actors exert "political-economic-cultural" control over unions in the Third World. According to this perspective: "imperialist activities are not necessarily confined to government actors or their agents: imperialist activities can be initiated by nongovernmental organizations (NGOs; such as labor organizations), based on their own analysis and arising out of intra-organizational dynamics, and they may or may not subsequently subordinate themselves to the desires of government actors (Ibid)."

In summarising the various features of labour imperialism, Rahman and Langford (2014, p. 173) note there are five essential hallmarks of trade union imperialism, namely:

> 1. Multiplication of trade unions (since imperialist labour organisation prefer to control affiliates rather than work with established unions; Southall 1995, p. 44). 2. Use of international financial resources to create clientele relations with the leaders and members of affiliates (Scipes 2010a, p. 37, 97; and Southall 1995, p. 45). 3. Failure to support the campaigns of leftist unions (this is a continuation of the anti-communism of the Cold War; Scipes 2010a, p. 92). 4. Support for bureaucratic avenues of change rather than mass actions by workers (Scipes 2010a, p. 111). 5. Promotion of Southern workers' rights and struggles in ways that can plausibly be interpreted as protectionism for Northern workers (Southall 1995, p. 45).

The presence of any of these factors in a circumstance where US labour interests or government interests have been involved indicates that a labour movement has been subject to hegemonic domination. In the subsequent sections, we will demonstrate that SEWA displays many of these hallmarks. Due to the historical record of the US labour movement and the US government regarding its interference with Third World labour movements, Scipes concludes that:

> *Until a detailed understanding of what they are doing in each particular country in which they are operating can be developed, evidence developed to date suggests that any overseas operations by the AFL-CIO, ACILS, or any other operation related to the AFL-CIO, the National Endowment for Democracy (NED), and/or the U.S. Government must be considered "guilty" of labor imperialism until proven innocent.* (2010a, p. 215)

A primary concern regarding SEWA is its links with US imperialist organisations and political figures. Pathak (2013) has conducted journalistic research on SEWA's overseas donations under the Foreign Contributions Regulation Act 2010. Because of this research, several key SEWA donors were revealed which included many imperialist institutions. These include The Rockefeller Foundation, the Ford Foundation, the World Bank, USAID, the Gates Foundation, the MacArthur Foundation, Women's World Banking, and the Embassies of the United States, Australia, Ireland and Switzerland amongst others.

Beyond Pathak's research, there is evidence that SEWA works with the US imperialist trade union network, the Solidarity Centre which is an arm of the AFL-CIO (Solidarity Centre 2013a). It is notable for example that in 1994 SEWA applied for funding from the United States' international aid arm, USAID soliciting support for SEWA bank (National Institute of Urban Affairs 1994). Further ties between SEWA, USAID, the Solidarity Centre and WIEGO (Women in Informal Employment Globalizing and Organising) can be seen in joint research projects sponsored by USAID and the Solidarity Centre (Solidarity Centre 2013b) and (WIEGO 2012). Scipes (2010a, p. 94) noted that USAID "is the agency through which the U.S. Government channeled millions of dollars throughout the 1960s and 1970s to AIFLD and parallel labour institutes in Africa and Asia." By SEWA's admission they have received funding from the World Bank, the Ford Foundation as well as Indian private sector organisations such as the Indian Tobacco Company, the Tech Mahindra Foundation and the Sir Dorabji Tata Trust (ILO 2011).

In a similar vein, SEWA has demonstrated that it has no qualms about aiding key figures and projects of US imperialism. Former US Secretary of State Hillary Clinton, for example, met SEWA representatives including their leaders twice in India, even celebrating the organisation in her book (Clinton 2004, pp. 280–1), and SEWA's currently leader Reema Nanavaty frequently visits the United States to consult with the US government and seek funding from various donors. Here we can observe the clientele relationship between SEWA and either the US government or the US labour movement. Despite claiming to be an apolitical organisation, SEWA also has no qualms about direct participation in the US imperialist project. In 2015, SEWA received a large USAID grant for work to set up vocational skills training programs in Afghanistan (USAID 2015).

Finally, a note of caution should be issued concerning microcredit as a progressive institution. A critical aspect of SEWA's work is SEWABANK, one of India's largest microcredit organisations. Muhammad (2015) has documented the case of Grameen Bank in Bangladesh as an example of how microfinance is directly connected to neoliberalism. Mader (2014, p. 137) argues that microcredit is not just "small sums of money handled in basic transactions," but is "part of a system of finance recognisable to other systems of finance. Microfinance is not the same as money lending or pawn brokering; it is financially more advanced, in that it incorporates the calculatory devices, languages and logics of the mainstream financial system into the act of lending to poor people."

In addition to this, Mahajan (2005) has demonstrated that microcredit has no impact on a nation's overall economic growth, and there is evidence that it has negative impacts on both innovation and job creation (Surowiecki 2008). While the Grameen Bank Initiative in Bangladesh has been widely praised in mainstream development circles leading to an expansion of microcredit schemes, a study by Jahiruddin et al. (2011) demonstrated that poor women are susceptible to failing businesses, and a cycle of debt dependency flowing from microcredit. In India, to date, the only published studies concerning microcredit are from people with close links to SEWA (Bhatt and Bhatt 2016) and as reporting submitted to USAID (Chen and Snodgrass 1999).

As noted by Muhammad (2015), microcredit also has a crucial role in advancing the neoliberal consensus by attacking the idea of the "state's responsibility to its citizens". Under this model "The state has taken the backseat. Structural reforms (for example, land reforms and institutional reforms) have been replaced by structural adjustment under the Washington Consensus." Rather than critique the structural sources of poverty, groups like SEWA attempt poverty alleviation without addressing its cause. We will now turn to examine SEWA's ideology.

Ideology of SEWA

Marcuse (2015) has argued that cooperatives are a viable institution on the path to socialism. They demonstrate the ability of workers to run their organisations, and thus the irrelevance of capitalists to the productive process (Ibid). "Co-ops today are experiments whose potential is not yet exhausted, certainly improvements over most existing capitalist arrangements which have perhaps portents for the future, but which have limitations that must be recognised (Ibid)." In discussing SEWA, it is to these limitations that we now turn.

Ratner, in a comparative study of the cooperative movement in the United States against Nanjie village in China, argued that cooperatives as a model of organization are not necessarily an alternative to capitalism, or even neoliberal capitalism (Ratner 2015). Instead, he argued that cooperatives can be compatible with neoliberalism noting that the foundational principles of cooperatives and transnational corporations are not necessarily different (Ibid). Ratner's argument demonstrates the importance of the ideological moorings of a cooperative organisation in determining whether it is a force for capital accumulation, working-class progress, or a transition toward socialism. It is in this light that we study SEWA.

In this section, we will argue that SEWA follows an ideology of liberal entrepreneurialism. We argue this is one of the main reasons SEWA has been able to attract the support of various capitalistic and imperialist backers, such as USAID, the Ford Foundation, the World Bank and the AFL-CIO's solidarity centre.

To understand the roots of SEWA ideology, some historical context is required. SEWA emerged from a split in the Textile Labour Association which was founded by MK Gandhi and Anasuya Sarabhai in 1920. Gandhi's model of unionism is class collaborationist in character as revealed by his 1920 statement on founding the TLA that "if you want to truly serve the workers, you should have regard for the interest of both the workers and the mill-owners...By establishing unions, we do not wish to intimidate the mill-owners but to protect the workers and we certainly have the rights to do this."

Ela Bhatt (2010), the founder of SEWA, describes herself as a Gandhian. As the founder of SEWA, as well as a long-serving president and thought leader, Bhatt's statements are revealing and reflective of SEWA's ideological approach.

As opposed to a critique of capitalism itself, Bhatt's approach singles out certain strata of Indian society, for example, the police, money lenders, government officials and intermediaries as being obstacles to the progress of the poor women whom SEWA organise (Ibid). In Bhatt's vision, capitalism is not the cause of poverty, rather by integrating SEWA women into capitalism through institutions such as microfinance, and a capitalistic labour market unburdened by social stigma, their position can be improved (Ibid).

Bhatt's (2012) statement that "The best innovations are often obvious ones. SEWA's innovation is thinking of poor women as resourceful workers who produce wealth for themselves, for other citizens and the nation."

demonstrates that she and SEWA do not have a problem with capitalism or global imperialism, which legitimates their strategy of broad donation acceptance including from powerful US imperialist interests.

This set of assumptions also leads SEWA to promote social entrepreneurship as a strategy to support the working poor. Bhatt suggests that "Social enterprise is not a project. It is a way of thinking so that society and economy can both benefit. The main feature is to focus on both, not just one, in all activities and results." In this statement, we observe a functionalist understanding of Indian society which is hugely like that espoused by Gandhi. Under this understanding, conflict within capitalism is an unnatural and avoidable thing.

Spodek (1994, p. 195) has argued that "much of SEWA's growth comes from its ability to work in alliance with different parties at various levels of government". While Spodek did not intend this, it is indeed a statement of indictment. It is now widely accepted that India's various political parties have almost entirely accepted the logic of neoliberal capitalism, either on a normative basis or based on an argument that there is no alternative. In working with these parties in a non-partisan way, SEWA demonstrates its compatibility with this framework.

Despite its claims to be a trade union, SEWA's approach is more consistent with that of an NGO, and its ideology is consistent with the neoliberal project. There are numerous concerns with the way that SEWA operates its construction cooperatives. Poor safety conditions, low wages, and an active attempt to depoliticize its workers were all things we witnessed first-hand. Our overall argument in this chapter is that these findings can be understood by way of SEWA's ideology and its associated NGO approach.

One of the most notable things about SEWA's ideology is that it offers no critique of capitalism. Most SEWA's efforts are spent in developing the capacities of SEWA members and attempting to integrate them into the capitalist market. It's analysis of social structures uses market language, which can be seen in their discussion of caste, class and gender issues which are conceptualised as 'barriers to entry' in the market economy (Bhatt 2015), rather than structural sources of disadvantage.

Frequent claims are made that SEWA luminaries have contributed to feminism (Moghadam 2015, p. 380; Spodek 1994; Ackerley and Okin 1999; Rose 1992; Bumiller 1990; Selliah 1989) as a movement. During the interviews, we asked the SEWA activists if as a movement of women, they discuss feminism or women's rights with their members. We were surprised that even among the educated activists, many didn't know what feminism was.

> We do not discuss feminism or the broader women's movement. We discuss specific trade issues or policies, and what SEWA is suggesting but not feminism. We do not even involve ourselves in domestic problems...if we hear of these issues...I give these issues to another organisation... Women have become so empowered that they become leaders in their communities, so if there are domestic problems they can solve the issue, but SEWA themselves do not talk about domestic issues. We do talk about sexual harassment in the workplace, but we do not talk about domestic issues. In a way, we can call ourselves feminists because we do create skills and the conditions for self-reliance. However, we do not go and propagate these ideas. (Field Notes, Interview Participant Anonymized 2015)

In this statement, made by an upper-level SEWA activist we can see the acceptance of the public-private sphere distinction, a clear suggestion of liberal ideology.

Even though it is a registered trade union, SEWA displays all the hallmarks of an NGO. While it does receive contributions from members, it is mainly dependent on private donations and funding from government departments which are unwilling or unable to perform their statutory responsibilities (Blaxall 2004, p. 2).

SEWA activists admitted that they operated on the same terms as an NGO regarding seeking donations, in that they were open to donations from almost any source. While SEWA were unwilling to disclose their list of donors, there is some evidence available about SEWA's activity in both seeking and receiving donations from questionable sources which should be noted as these demonstrate the overall ideological approach of SEWA as well as demonstrate potential sources of leverage which various forces have over its activities.

SEWA historiography concerning its microcredit arm, SEWA Bank, portrays a glorious story of self-organization. The truth about SEWA exposes that from its very inception, SEWA has been dependent on donations and foreign funding. The accepted canon of SEWA Bank history suggests that 4000 members initially contributed 10rs to found the bank, giving the bank an estimated working capital of 40,000rs (ILO 2011, p. 145) which by 2006 has become some 94 crore rupees (940,000,000rs). Even when allowing for the growth of SEWA's membership and the associated expansion of deposits to the bank, the idea that this amount materialised through the

Table 5.1 SEWA total recorded foreign funding

Year	*Contribution Total (Rs)*	*Estimated Total (2017 $US)*
2011–12	249,079,746	3,655,395
2010–11	309,272,887	4,538,766
2009–10	242,525,566	3,559,208
2008–09	245,571,883	3,603,915
2007–08	183,063,291	2,686,564
2006–07	176,194,772	2,585,764

normal workings of the bank is implausible, meaning the bank has most likely received significant foreign donations either directly or indirectly through other SEWA conduits.

Foreign contributions to SEWA based on the Foreign Contributions Regulations Act data demonstrated that SEWA received foreign donations to its various arms. Table 5.1 demonstrates yearly contributions to SEWA as examples.

The next crucial stage of SEWA's work is its move beyond India. SEWA has had essential impacts in shaping political developments in other countries, but also at the international level. Part of SEWA's expansion involves the creation of new SEWA organisations, which has taken place in Turkey, Yemen and South Africa not by working with the existing labour movements but by establishing new organisations (Baruah 2011, p. 11). Thus it can be seen that once the hegemonic effect of this type of organisation is set up in one country, it spreads to countries with similar conditions.

The next significant step in this involves the creation of the NGO Women in Informal Employment Globalizing and Organizing (WIEGO), an organisation which SEWA played a major part in forming. WIEGO's NGO work attempts to conduct research and advocacy work reflecting SEWA and other similar organisations' perspective on the international stage, such as through the mainstream trade union movement, or the arms of the United Nations including the International Labor Organization. Notably, WIEGO is also sponsored by the Solidarity Centre and USAID (Solidarity Centre 2013b).

On the level of the organisation, therefore, there appear to be several reasons to be skeptical or critical of SEWA's approach to working class organisation which has not yet been addressed in the academic literature and which warrant further discussion and investigation. We believe that SEWA's approach demonstrates the flexibility and compatibility of cooperative models of organisation and neoliberal capitalism insofar as cooperatives are not imbibed with a progressive and transformative political agenda. However, we also feel it is necessary to demonstrate the grassroots impact which SEWA. To this end, we will now turn to a case study of the SEWA Rachaita Construction Cooperative.

History of SEWA Rachaita

The history of SEWA as an organisation has been extensively covered elsewhere (Rose 1995; Saini 2007, p. 821) and thus we will not focus on this here, instead preferring to concentrate on the history of the construction worker's cooperative which we studied through our research. SEWA first began organising women construction workers in 1998 (SEWA 2012, p. 20). The political economy surrounding SEWA Rachaita's formation concerned the deindustrialization of the textile industry in Gujarat. This occurred as a result of liberalisation measures initiated in the sector from 1985 onwards as well as India's general liberalisation measures beginning in 1991 (Howell and Kambhampati 2007, p. 112). This exposed the industry to international competition and led to a wave of plant closures and a shedding of labour (Ibid). This period was important in the history of both SEWA and SEWA Rachaita as it significantly changed the working dynamics in the region, and expanded SEWA's base of organising.

> When the textile mills started to close, the women were the first to be retrenched, with their money many became street vendors, those with skills became screen painters, those with no money become waste collectors...the SEWA leaders brought up the issue of the contract workers...this led to the creation of a contract labour committee. From this committee, it was decided to form a construction workers cooperative. (Field Notes 2015)

The initial establishment of the cooperative was a painful process. Construction work has been male-dominated in India and women when they are involved, usually play the role of 'helpers' carrying materials so that men can do the construction.

> To convince the government that women construction workers can form their cooperative was difficult. The Government did not believe that this could happen. After we got registered, we had no experience of contracts, so it was difficult to get tenders. We were not taken seriously at first. At first, we got given cleaning work, and general unskilled work, grass cutting work.

> We would clear a work site based on the promise of being able to take the contract and then denied the contract. (Field Notes 2015)

SEWA Rachaita's first construction contract came when SEWA negotiated their first contract with the Bakeri construction company, which importantly also provided training to the workers before commencing the contract. For the first time, SEWA's construction teams would get the responsibility for the construction tasks which had historically been done by men. This would bring up its own set of challenges.

> The first problem was the clothes they would wear, particularly while working on scaffolds. The men would tease and eve-tease the women. We had to change the way women dressed...changing their mindset was tough. We brought salwar from our own homes and made them wear it. After hearing the criticism from the men, the women lost confidence. They relied on the support from other women. (Field Notes 2015)

The skills learned through the Bakeri project enabled SEWA Rachaita to begin its record as a company. The lack of experience and track record had been a significant obstacle in negotiating for tenders. In addition to this, the relatively unskilled workforce led many companies to question the ability of SEWA Rachaita to complete the projects to the required standards successfully. Because of the Bakeri project, SEWA could train their first batch of master trainers, who received accreditation and could pass on their skills to other workers (Field Notes 2015).

Despite our overall criticism of SEWA, its ideology and its approach, the positive impact which this successful project had on many of the women workers we met should not be understated. One significant achievement of SEWA was to help break down the patriarchal mindset in the construction industry through their example of successful work.

> My husband used to say you cannot work like this, the SEWA people are just ruining you, the SEWA women do not know anything and just say go, but you will not be able to do it, you cannot make the contract on your own... now I've become the supervisor, and he has to ask me where to go for work. (Field Notes 2015)

Structure of SEWA Rachaita

Significant work has been done documenting SEWA's overall structure. In this section, we will focus on the structure of SEWA's Rachaita Construction cooperative to give an idea of how the organisation is designed and the impact this organisational design has on the overall function and philosophy of the cooperative.

To join SEWA Rachaita, SEWA members must pay a fee to become 'shareholders' in the cooperative. At the time of interviewing this fee was 100rs, which is approximately US$2. Upon paying this fee, members are entitled to a full and equal share of dividends (if any) (Field Notes 2015).

Regarding the leadership structure, for every 50 construction workers, there is one leader who is elected on a 3-yearly basis by members. Above this structure is a trade committee which is made up of all the leaders. Each trade committee elects members to the representative committee which elects the SEWA executive committee (Field Notes 2015).

Running parallel to this leadership structure, however, is the supervisory structure. Each worksite has a 'supervisor' who is appointed top-down by SEWA's cooperative coordinator. This supervisor has control over the distribution of work and training opportunities to cooperative members, which as will be discussed below, is significant as it largely determines which members are promoted, receive higher salaries and in many cases who can obtain work and when (Field Notes 2015).

While this structure appears broadly democratic, there are significant ways in which SEWA's executive leadership retains control over the process. During one of our site visits to a SEWA construction site, we observed one of the leaders disciplining a cooperative member who had come to work. The leader alleged that the worker had not regularly attended work and thus the worker was excluded from participation in the worksite and was not being paid (Field Notes 2015).

In interviewing the people in leadership positions, it immediately became apparent that these people had very long-term associations with SEWA to the extent that this appeared a necessary 'qualification' to become a leader. One worksite leader had been a member of SEWA for 30 years, and a member of the construction cooperative for seven years, including as a founding member. This person has been a supervisor for the entire time and had previously also worked with SEWA as an organiser. The construction workers and even the SEWA activists admitted that they had never had a contested election for political leadership positions with the workers approving whoever is nominated by SEWA (Field Notes 2015).

Given this, we can see that while SEWA has a relatively democratic structure, it lacks a democratic culture regarding the running of its cooperatives which has a significant impact on the cooperative regarding its economic democracy as well. The construction workers suggested that they had rarely been paid dividends for their participation in the cooperative, and suggested they knew little about the overall running of the cooperative from a business standpoint. The workers had no idea how much money the contracts were worth, how much was spent on operating costs, and how much of that money was paid to SEWA for administration costs. This lack knowledge and transparency when coupled with the fact that the workers were being paid lower than both the statutory minimum as well as the market rates of pay, as will be discussed in the next section, were a source of concern.

Work and Working Conditions

The working conditions of the construction workers in the cooperative were deplorable. We visited a construction site and observed the team of women working without safety equipment of any kind. They were lifting and using heavy equipment in 'chappals' (in Australia we call them thongs, in the US they are flip flops). The irony of this situation is that the work site had various safety warning signs suggesting among other things that proper footwear should be worn. Many of the privately-run construction work teams on the site had workers with proper footwear and safety equipment, which demonstrates that it is not necessarily the prevailing norm to ignore safety requirements (Field Notes and Site Observation 2015).

India's Contract Labour Abolition and Regulation Act 1970 (Labour Resources Department 1970) states amongst other things that contract workers in India should be paid at the wage rates set by the government should be provided with facilities such as spaces for latrines, drinking water, washing, first aid. While a failure to comply with this Act is widespread across the Indian informal sector, it is notable that SEWA as a trade union is a standard setter. Its failure to ensure compliance with the Act on its worksites sends a signal that is heard across the labour market and casts doubt on its claims to raise the standard of living of its members. Interviews with workers revealed that SEWA Cooperative workers are required to fetch their own water, there were no facilities provided on site and insufficient wages (Field Notes 2015).

The salary of the workers was meagre, below both the prevailing minimum wage rate for the construction industry in Gujarat as well as the market rate for construction work. Unskilled workers, known as 'helpers' would receive wages of 300rs per day with semi-skilled 'masters' being paid 550rs per day. A supervisor (normally one of the more experienced 'masters') would receive a premium of 235rs per day on top of their wage and is provided transport to the worksite (Field Notes 2015).

In seeking to explain the lower rates of pay, both the workers and the leaders offered similar explanations which suggest that the hold of SEWA ideology over its membership is a crucial reason behind the lower rates of pay (Field Notes 2015). Firstly, there is a narrative which provides a critique of Indian social values, suggesting these to be a barrier to higher rates of pay. Within SEWA's overall narrative there is an emphasis on so-called 'conceptual blocks' (Rose 1995, p. 45) which need to be overcome to improve the status of self-employed women. This logic has been extended to the construction cooperatives where SEWA leaders argue that many construction companies refuse to admit that women can be construction workers in the full sense, rather than just performing rudimentary tasks such as the provision of water or head loading bulky objects.

In negotiations with work contractors, SEWA leaders argued that the trade-off for these conceptual blocks is that SEWA had to offer lower cost contracts to convince companies to sign the contracts with SEWA. This appears to lock the women's construction cooperatives into a permanent state of lower pay.

Secondly, SEWA members emphasised the role of the cooperative as a safer space. In this sense, the members are articulating a trade-off between the higher wages of the private sector, against the lower wages of the cooperative sector with its benefit of a less patriarchal environment.

> Outside the cooperatives, there's no women's unity, here we are all sisters, and look after each other, there we get harassed by men. Here the monthly salary is paid, and there we get day wages. We get respect in our society, and our household ...we can teach our daughters and children. (Field Notes 2015)

The workers informed us of several other problems regarding their work with the cooperative. In most cases, workers needed to find some alternative form of employment along with the cooperative work. This ordinarily involved work as day labourers in the private construction labour market which exists in Ahmedabad. Additionally, the workers admitted that they were not always able to find employment and were periodically unemployed because of their participation in the cooperative. There were also transitional problems due to the contractual nature of the construction cooperative. Large projects typically lasted between 1 to 1.5 years, and at the end of these projects, there were periodic bouts of unemployment (Field Notes 2015).

(Dis)Empowerment

An additional aspect of SEWA's approach was observed in the various site visits we undertook. We are broadly grouping these under the heading of 'disempowerment' for what we hope will be self-evident reasons.

SEWA's cooperative leaders noted that one of the first aspects of conditioning SEWA members to work in the construction cooperative was their deradicalization. The leaders pointed out that the women often came from experiences of more militant trade unions, or with this perception in mind, or from one of SEWA's earlier struggles. Upon joining the cooperatives, they retained this militancy, and it was argued that an active campaign was necessary to convince the women to behave like business people instead of like workers to create a successful cooperative (Field Notes 2015).

In SEWA's terms, we, therefore, see an oppositional framework set up between the idea of working-class militancy and the idea of successful cooperative enterprises. This profoundly troubling experience helps illustrate the role that SEWA ideology plays in shaping the strategy and tactics used in the cooperatives. One SEWA leader went so far as to say "I do not know why we need trade unions, we should just organise all women into cooperatives" (Field Notes 2015).

The second aspect to note is that SEWA leaders were fully against the provision of political education to their members. One activist argued that "We tell them about the laws, we say that we are lobbying and advocating, but we never do political education. We are not a political organisation, so we do not discuss politics" (Field Notes 2015). Government policies at all levels of government, as well as internationally, have a significant impact on SEWA members and yet as a union/cooperative body, the organisation takes the position that politics is not something worth discussing with its members.

Finally, as has already been discussed, there have been several people who have argued that SEWA's leadership and the organisation itself have made substantial contributions to feminism. While the top leadership of SEWA have made public comments about women's rights and about feminism, the level of discourse when observing the relationship between SEWA leaders and SEWA workers is altogether different. When asked to comment on feminism, one high ranking SEWA policy officer noted that:

> We do not discuss feminism or the broader women's movement with the workers. We discuss specific trade issues or policies, and what SEWA is suggesting but not feminism. We do not even involve ourselves in domestic problems…if

> we take up these issues…I give these issues to another organisation. Women have become so empowered that they become leaders in their communities, so if there are domestic problems they can solve the issue, but SEWA themselves do not talk about domestic issues. We do talk about sexual harassment in the workplace, but we do not talk about domestic issues. In a way, we can call ourselves feminists because we do create skills and the conditions for self-reliance. However, we do not go and propagate these ideas. (Field Notes 2015)

In addition to the active avoidance of feminist discourse within the SEWA movement, this statement is revealing. It demonstrates that SEWA implicitly accepts the public-private distinction, a long-criticised dichotomy within feminist politics and a bastion of liberal thought.

Recalling the discussion of labour imperialism by Rahman and Langford (2014, p. 173), they listed the failure to support leftist unions and their campaigns, along with bureaucratic methods of change as critical hallmarks of unions which have been hegemonized by trade union imperialism. SEWA's claims to non-participation in politics should be seen in this light.

Conclusion

Until now, SEWA has received almost universal praise for its activities in organising poor 'self-employed' women in India. In this chapter, we have argued that there are many reasons for skepticism of SEWA which require further exploration. SEWA's links with capitalistic and imperialistic organisations have not been properly scrutinised, by proponents of progressive politics who seem all too keen to embrace SEWA and its methods as the answer to globalisation. SEWA's ideology lends itself to a kind of 'yellow' unionism which supports and reinforces neoliberal capitalist ideology through its theory and practice.

SEWA's methods at best perpetuate a permanent state of informality within the Indian working class, a theory that is now being advanced by left apologists for globalisation under the rubric that there is no alternative to neoliberal globalisation. We have aimed to demonstrate that SEWA's practice through its cooperative movement is a practice which encourages unsafe workspaces, low wages, a depoliticized working environment and a depoliticized woman worker. Far from being the radical solution of the future or the empowerment of the working class, we have argued that SEWA represent a force favouring neoliberal capitalism.

References

Ackerley, Brooke and Okin, Susan. 1999. Feminist Social Criticism and the International Movement for Women's Rights as Human Rights. In, Shapiro, Ian and Hacker-Cordon, Casiano. *Democracy's Edges*. Cambridge University Press: Cambridge.

Agarwala, R. 2013. *Informal labor, formal politics and dignified discontent in India*. New York: Cambridge University Press.

Baruah, Bipasha. 2011. *Women and Property in Urban India*. UBC Press: Toronto.

Bhatt, Amola and Bhatt, Shahir. 2016. Microfinancing with SEWA Bank: Bringing Women to the Mainstream Economy. *Amity Business Review*. Vol 17, No 1.

Bhatt, Ela. 2010. *A Discussion with Ela Bhatt, Founder, Self-Employed Women's Association (SEWA)*. Available from: https://berkleycenter.georgetown.edu/interviews/a-discussion-with-ela-bhatt-founder-self-employed-women-s-association-sewa

Bhatt, Ela. 2012. *Social Entrepreneurship: Innovation at the Service of Social Change*. Available from: http://www.iese.edu/es/files/Interview%202-%20Newsletter%2013_tcm5-75437.pdf

Bhatt, Ela. 2015. *SEWA Approaches to Poverty Removal*. Available from: http://www.sewa.org/Archives_Poverty_Removal.asp

Blaxall, J. 2004. India's Self-Employed Women's Association (SEWA): Empowerment Through Mobilization of Poor Women on a Large Scale. In Scaling Up Poverty Reduction: A Global Learning Process and Conference, Shanghai.

Bumiller, Elisabeth. 1990. *May You Be the Mother of a Hundred Sons: A Journey Among the Women of India*. New York: Fawcett Columbine.

Chen, Martha and Snodgrass, Donald. 1999. *An Assessment of the Impact of SEWA Bank in India: Baseline Findings*. Available from: http://pdf.usaid.gov/pdf_docs/Pnacg038.pdf

Clinton, Hillary. 2004. *Living History*. Simon and Schuster: New York.

Coe, Neil and Jordhus-Lier, David. 2010. Constrained Agency? Re-Evaluating the Geographies of Labour. *Progress in Human Geography*. Vol 35, No 2.

Datta, Rekha. 2003. From Development to Empowerment: The Self-Employed Women's Association in India. *International Journal of Politics, Culture and Society*. Vol 16, Iss 3. pp351–368

Gandhi, MK. 1920. *File Photo of Printed Statement in Gandhi Smarak Sangrahalaya*. Gandhi Museum: Ahmedabad.

Glassman, Jim. 2004. Transnational Hegemony and US Labor Foreign Policy: Towards a Gramscian International Labor Geography. *Environment and Planning Development: Society and Space*. Vol 22, No 4.

Hensman, Rohini. 2011. *Workers, Unions and Global Capitalism: Lessons from India*. Columbia University Press: New York.

Herod, A. 1997. From a geography of labor to a labor geography. *Antipode* 29, 1–31.

Herod, A (ed). 1998. *Organising the landscape.* Minneapolis, MN Minnesota University Press.

Herod, A. 2001. *Labor geographies.* New York: Guilford Press.

Howell, Jude and Kambhampati, Uma. 2007. Liberalization and Labour: The Fate of Retrenched Workers in the Cotton Textile Industry in India. *Oxford Development Studies.* Vol 27, No 1.

International Labour Organization. 2011. *Rural Employment and the Decent Work Program.* Available from: http://www.ilo.org/wcmsp5/groups/public/---ed_emp/---emp_policy/documents/publication/wcms_234890.pdf

Jahiruddin, ATM, Short, Patricia, Dressler, Wolfram and Khan, M Adil. 2011. Can Microcredit Worsen Poverty? Cases of Exacerbated Poverty in Bangladesh. *Development in Practice.* Vol 21, No 8.

Kerswell, Timothy and Pratap, Surendra. 2017. Labour imperialism in India: The case of SEWA. *Geoforum.* Vol 85: 20–22.

Labour Resources Department: Government of India. 1970. *The Contract Labour (Regulation and Abolition) Act, 1970.* Available from: http://labour.bih.nic.in/Acts/contract_labour_regulation_and_abolition_act_1970.pdf

Mader, Phillip. 2014. *The Political Economy of Microfinance: Financializing Poverty.* London: Palgrave.

Mahajan, Vijay. 2005. From Microcredit to Livelihood Finance. *Economic and Political Weekly.* Vol 40, No 41.

Marcuse, Peter. 2015. Cooperatives on the Path to Socialism? *Monthly Review.* Vol 66, Iss 9.

Moghadam, Val. 2015. Gender and Globalization: Female Labour and Women's Mobilization. *Journal of World-Systems Research.* Vol 5, Iss 2.

Muhammad, Anu. 2015. Bangladesh – A Model of Neoliberalism: The Case of Microfinance and NGOs. *Monthly Review.* Vol 66, Iss 10.

National Institute of Urban Affairs. 1994. *Analysis: Down Marketing Housing Finance Through Community Based Financial Systems.* Available from: http://pdf.usaid.gov/pdf_docs/PNABZ402.pdf

Pathak, Japan K. 2013. *Imagine the figure of foreign money received by SEWA organizations, then read the actual number!* Available from: http://deshgujarat.com/2013/05/26/imagine-the-figure-of-foreign-money-recieved-by-sewa-organizations-then-read-the-actual-number/

Radosh, Ronald. 1969. *American Labor and United States Foreign Policy.* New York: Random House.

Rahman, Zia and Langford, Tom. 2014. International Solidrarity or Renewed Trade Union Imperialism? The AFL-CIO and Garment Workers in Bangladesh. *WorkingUSA: The Journal of Labor and Society.* Vol 17.

Ratner, Carl. 2015. Neoliberal Cooptation of Leading Coop Organizations, and a Socialist Counter-Politics of Cooperation. *Monthly Review.* Vol 66, Iss 9.

Rose, K. 1992. *Where women are leaders: The SEWA movement in India.* London: Zed Books.

Rose, Kalima. 1995. *Where Women are Leaders: The SEWA Movement in India*. Zed Books: London.

Saini, Debi S. 2007. Securing Working Class Rights For Informal Sector Workers In India: A Case Study Of Self-Employed Women's Association. *The Indian Journal of Labour Economics*. Vol 50, No 4. P821

Schmidt, George. 1978. *The American Federation of Teachers and the CIA*. Chicago: Substitutes United for Better Schools.

Scipes, Kim. 2010a. *AFL-CIO's Secret War against Developing Country Workers: Solidarity or Sabotage?* Lanham MD: Lexington Books

Scipes, Kim. 2010b. Why Labor Imperialism? AFL-CIO's Foreign Policy Leaders and the Developing World. *WorkingUSA: The Journal of Labor and Society*. Vol 13, No 4.

Scott, Jack. 1978. *Yankee Unions, Go Home!: How the AFL Helped the US Build an Empire in Latin America*. Vancouver: New Star Books.

Selliah, S. 1989. *The Self-Employed Women's Association, Ahmedabad, India*. Geneva: International Labour Office.

SEWA. 2012. *SEWA Annual Report 2012*. Available from: http://www.sewa.org/pdf/SEWA-ANNUAL-REPORT-2012.pdf

Solidarity Centre. 2013a. *Workshop Women Workers Organizing: Examples from India, Brazil and Liberia*. Available from: http://www.solidaritycenter.org/workshop-women-workers-organizing-examples-from-india-brazil-and-liberia/

Solidarity Centre. 2013b. The *Transformation of Work: Challenges and Strategies*. Available from: http://www.solidaritycenter.org/wp-content/uploads/2014/11/WIEGO.Informal-Workers-and-Collective-Bargaining.pdf

Southall, R. 1995. *Imperialism or Solidarity? International Labour and South African Trade Unions*. Rondelbosch: University of Cape Town Press.

Spodek, Howard. 1994. Review Article: The Self-Employed Women's Association (SEWA) in India: Feminist, Gandhian Power in Development. *Economic Development and Cultural Change*. Vol 43, Iss 1.

Surowiecki, James. 2008. What Microloans Miss. *The New Yorkers*. March 17. Available from: http://www.newyorker.com/magazine/2008/03/17/what-microloans-miss

Thomson, Don and Larson, Rodney. 1978. *Where were you, brother? An Account of Trade Union Imperialism*. London: War on Want.

USAID. 2015. *India and US to Strengthen Livelihoods of Over 3000 Afghan Women*. Available from: https://www.usaid.gov/india/press-releases/may-8-2015-india-and-us-strengthen-livelihoods-over-3000-afghan-women

WIEGO. 2012. *Collective Bargaining by Workers of the Indian Unorganized Sector: Struggle, Process, Achievements, and Learning*. Available from: http://wiego.org/sites/wiego.org/files/resources/files/Collective-Bargaining-%20India.pdf

Wills, J. 1998. Taking on the Cosomocorps? Experiments in Transnational Labour Organization. *Economic Geography*. Vol 74.

CHAPTER 6

Neoliberalism vs. Village Collectivism: A Success Story from an Indian Village

Since the onset of its liberalisation policy framework in 1994, India's workers and peasants have faced a rapidly deteriorating situation. Various policy prescriptions from neoliberalism to orthodox Marxism suggest that there are no alternatives to capitalistic development and therefore the proletarianization and urbanisation of India's population. These policy prescriptions have generated crises in employment and agriculture, as well as avoid in alternatives.

In this chapter, we discuss the struggle of Menda Lekha village in Maharashtra, India which has struggled to build an alternative development through the creation of collective farming and democratic methods. We will demonstrate how the village leaders capitalised on a wave of politicisation around an anti-dam movement, to transform the village and its structures of ownership and social relations. In doing so, they created a useful model of resistance against the mainstream policies of development.

India is facing a severe challenge of poverty, unemployment, underemployment, precarious, unhealthy working, living environments and social exclusion. The neoliberal governments, politicians, academics as well as various national and international institutions forcefully argue that these problems are due to a lack of development. There are no alternatives other than achieving high growth and urbanisation rates, expanding the urban consumer middle class, shrinking agriculture and shifting the agrarian population to cities.

T. Kerswell, S. Pratap, *Worker Cooperatives in India*,
https://doi.org/10.1007/978-981-13-0384-5_6

Policies within this framework include a common framework. Therefore, policies and strategies are developed based on some common factors. Commoditization, privatisation, and corporatization of all resources, fully opening the economy to national and international capital, no support or protection to producers and traders, the free international mobility of capital and goods; and attracting substantial foreign direct investment and boosting exports.

Promoting individualism, consumerism and competition among labourers and consumers in society are part of this strategy. However, rather than resolving all the problems, these policies and strategies have made them worse. Poverty and unemployment are reaching the dangerous levels, mainly because large-scale drives for urbanisation have destroyed more livelihoods than they have created. A vast population is forced to work and live in precarious conditions. Also increasing to alarming levels are the health and safety problems, where the people themselves are blamed for their conditions and preached to work hard, adopt 'good habits' and practice cleanliness. The state offers some good sounding welfare schemes that mean nothing more than another active form of capital accumulation.

The discourse which currently dominates the whole political, economic, social and cultural environment in India that either fully justifies the policies and strategies or accepts them because there are no alternatives. The social and political movements that are challenging these strategies are scattered and weak, but most importantly, they are not projecting any practical and viable alternative.

Against this background, this study explores the social experiments of Menda village, which has built an alternative model of development at a microscopic level but with broader significance. In doing so, it has vigorously challenged the dominant discourse on strategies of development. Menda is a small tribal village located in the forests of the Gadchiroli district of Maharashtra. The villagers began creating new development dynamics after experiencing a political awakening during a series of anti-dam protests.

They did this by first looking back at their history and gradually conceptualised an understanding of the cause of all present-day problems including a lack of care for the conservation of natural resources, private property, individualism, alcoholism and democracy based on majoritarianism. The villagers argued that these factors destroy the very basis of survival, therefore creating a division among the people. By this conceptualization, they gradually moved towards practising a new development model along with new ways of working and living based on collectivity and democracy. According to the results of the policies, distress migration stopped, and incomes increased while most have escaped the poverty trap. Also, the education level has been increasing along with a visible improvement in living and working conditions.

We base our discussion of the movement and various developments in Menda on extensive interviews with the leader of Menda Gram Sabha (village council), Devaji Tofa and Charan Das Tofa, who looks after documentation and accounts of the Gram Sabha, along with interviews with other families in the village. We complemented the interview data with observations that took place during site visits observing developments in the village. Further to this, we have relied on studies conducted by other researchers to corroborate the historical perspectives provided by the interviewees.

The chapter begins by outlining the orthodox development strategies with particular reference to India. The current example of this is the Modi government's 'Make in India' framework, but we argue that there has been a little significant change in approach since India's liberalisation.

Current development strategies, whether those adopted by the nationalist right or the Marxist left, are based on the false premise of the European experience of capitalism as a universal experience. This assumption and the associated policies compound pre-existing development problems rooted in India's history. The chapter then argues that Menda provides a case study of alternative possibilities of development rooted in a collectivist approach promoting the democratic management of development and rejecting the linear view of capitalist development, basing its strategies on particular local experiences.

Orthodox Strategies of Development: The Political Economy of 'Make in India'

The Make in India development strategy is not a new strategy; it is the same strategy followed in the last two decades of liberalisation. The new global politico-economic regime has already been able to form or force consent around these strategies among almost all Indian parliamentary parties from right to left, primarily based on the proposition that there is no alternative. However, the roar of the Make in India slogan certainly means that the current government is determined to aggressively continue on this road by forcefully removing all hurdles and ignoring or suppressing all the dissent. Therefore, the discussion on development strategy in this chapter begins with a brief critique of the development strategy adopted in the phase of liberalisation and globalisation.

India is a labour surplus country and its painful conditions along with vicious cycles of poverty have roots in development dynamics that have been unable to reduce or resolve the intensity of substantial labour reserves. The deindustrialisation and destruction of craft industries were the causes of this problem (Patnaik 2009). These acts expelled scores of traditional artisans into the ranks of labour reserves, typically located in agriculture and other low-paid occupations everywhere in the informal sector (Ibid). Capitalist development in India since its independence has been severely affected by this problem. The rural sector was unable to emerge as an effective market and thereby hindered industrial growth. Industrial growth was unable to generate significant employment and to ease the burden of surplus labour from agriculture, thereby hindering the capitalist development of the rural sector.

Some policy measures would have helped to address comprehensive land reforms, the equitable distribution of land and other natural resources among the rural population, industrial development based on developing indigenous technologies, and the promotion of labour-intensive manufacturing based on local resources and local market. These strategies were primarily ignored post-independence and constitute a significant factor behind the economy's systemic crisis in the late 1970s. At this point, we can observe the slow shift towards liberalisation in India based on the logic of the 'successful' experiences of the West in history.

Based on generalising the experiences of capitalist development in Europe, the United States, and in Japan, the neoliberal school of thought (Agarwala 2015), as well as the dominant discourse among the left, presumes that the capitalist expansion ultimately reduces poverty. It does so by generating vast employment opportunities in industries and absorbing petty economies (Marx and Engels 1975, p. 491). A related presumption is that capitalist development necessarily shifts the workforce from agriculture to industries, considered an indicator of capitalist development and a positive development regarding overall socio-economic development. The assumption behind this thinking is it will lead to the end of chronic poverty, with the inbuilt presumption that working and living conditions in agriculture are always bad in comparison to industries and cannot be improved.

Sanyal, for example, has argued that 'urbanisation is the sociological and spatial counterpart to economic processes that shift workers away from subsistence agriculture to more productive sectors. It is the physical manifestation of all the construction activity that accompanies rapid growth (2008, p. 193)'. The Planning Commission (2008, p. 394) echoes this argument by saying, 'Urbanisation is a key indicator of economic development and should be seen as a positive factor for overall development'. Since the Modi government took power, it has articulated normative urbanisation through the policy of 'smart cities' being developed across India (Make in India 2016).

The only difference in the left discourse is its emphasis that capitalist development leads to proletarianization and expands the reserve army of labour. Indian left discourse welcomes capitalist development and proletarianization as a necessary step towards socialism. Left discourse argues that petty economies create illusions and act as hurdles in developing a collective working class consciousness. Prakash Karat (2007), then General Secretary of the Communist Party of India (Marxist) (CPIM), for example, claimed opponents of CPIM's attempt to displace peasants in West Bengal for industrial development were modern-day 'Narodniks', a pejorative reference to agrarian socialists in pre-revolutionary Russia. The preceding analysis is part of a wider trend within Marxism known as productive force determinism, currently exemplified by China's development policy since the 'reform and opening' period. According to this perspective, a primary stage of socialism that necessitates an extended period of capitalist development, urbanisation and industrialisation as a necessary step toward socialism (Sun 1995, pp. 184–5; McCarthy 1985, p. 143; Dai 1987, p. 5).

In fact, capitalist development in India is not able to transcend these dynamics: Petty commodity production and economies dominate the scene with more than 50% of the workforce still surviving on agriculture. Accordingly, left discourse generally (Das 2010, p. 301; CPI (Maoist) 2004, p. 16) considers the Indian economy a pre-capitalist economy rather than a capitalist economy. This position mirrors the analysis of Lewis (1954), who argued that many post-colonial societies be a combination of traditional and modern economies.

The neoliberal school of thought proposes that achieving a high rate of economic growth is the only solution to unemployment and poverty. It strongly argues for the removal of all hurdles along the path of development at any cost, including the allegedly short-run cost of people's welfare. While the dominant left discourse questions some events that negatively affect the people, it accepts the 'need' for faster economic growth to resolve poverty and unemployment. They are unable to propose an alternative development strategy, instead of demanding capitalistic employment generation and arguing for inclusive growth (de Haan and Thoarat 2013, p. 2).

In the current phase of globalisation, with the integration of the national and global economy based on a new international division of labour, accompanied with a historic downfall in the working-class movements, the balance of power has decisively shifted in favour of capital. This is also clearly reflected in the rising share of profits and declining share of wages. The proportion of wages in the national income fell from 40% at the start of the 1990s to only 34% by 2009–2010 (UNCTAD 2012). In this phase, we observe a most aggressive form of capitalist expansion leading to large-scale expropriation, the mass destruction of livelihoods and dispossession from natural resources, like land, water and forests. In India, this is likely the first time in recent history that we can observe an absolute decline in the workforce engaged in agriculture. The capitalist expansion is also destructively moving to absorb various other sectors of small economies like fishing, retail trade along with waste collection and management.

However, the presumption that capitalist development ultimately alleviates poverty by creating ample wage employment opportunities, with better working conditions and earnings, which is only a myth. This conception emerges from a Eurocentric analysis of capitalism and its history in Europe, Japan and European settler colonies like the United States and Australia, which forms the basis of this generalisation. The modernization theory of Rostow (1960, p. 4) exemplifies this analysis, but overcoming Eurocentric analysis has been a fundamental problem in Marxism as well. Amin, for example, argued feudalism is a specifically European, rather than universal experience (Kerswell 2015, p. 6), and Biel claiming that Marxist writers have consistently struggled against the limitations of its Eurocentric origins (2015, p. 201).

The expansion of capital goes hand in hand with its concentration and centralization. The consistently increasing organic composition of capital in the form of rising levels of mechanisation and automation are integral to profit-maximizing strategies, resulting in the reserve army of labour's creation and expansion. All of these processes occurred in Europe as well. However, if the outcome of the capitalist development in Europe looks different, it is not because of the logic of capitalist development. Europe enjoyed two rare opportunities, (a) the large-scale outmigration of its population through the generation of settler colonial spaces; and (b) a monopoly on markets and natural resources through colonies. Patnaik (2011) argues that migration to settler colonies and the displacement of pre-colonial production systems were experiences unique to capitalism in Europe. From this, we should conclude that the analysis of capitalism in non-European countries should not be based on the idea of catching up with the West, but rather by addressing particular socio-historical conditions unique to non-imperialist countries.

The above discussion shows that capitalist expansion or a high rate of economic growth does not offer any significant prospects for resolving the problem of unemployment and poverty. It is not possible to 'catch up with the West' when the Western experience is both historically unique and impossible to replicate. It is thus essential to briefly discuss the development strategies based on a new international division of labour forming the basis of Make in India and critically look at the potential of Make in India regarding resolving the problems of unemployment and poverty.

The new global politico-economic regime enforces a new international division of labour by integrating global economies in such a way that it facilitates surplus appropriation at the global level without any boundaries and empowers metropolitan or imperialist capital to capture the major part of surplus generated worldwide. The free global movement of capital and goods and the free play of market are the rules of the game. National governments are required to deregulate finance, pricing, labour regulations, tariffs and agricultural subsidies (however, there are no significant restrictions in providing tax exemptions and incentives to capital, even if that is also a form of subsidy).

Supranational institutions like World Trade Organization (WTO), International Monetary Fund (IMF), World Bank and various regional and bilateral free trade agreements institutionalise and constitutionalize this new global governing system. The national government attempting to violate the above rule of the game may be dragged to the international courts and also invite various punishments from the IMF and WTO and economic sanctions from the metropolitan capital. However, there is another dynamic that compels the national states to follow the rules of the game.

Once the national economies have shifted to the path of Foreign Direct Investment-based export-oriented development, they are compelled to compete with many other national economies to offer better super profits to metropolitan capital to obtain more significant shares of FDI and exports. In a situation of unrestricted capital mobility, this becomes a continuous battle. The threat of capital flight forces them to fall in line and even go beyond this to offer better prospects for capital. In doing so, they do not gain control over the new technology due to the structuring of commodity chains by corporations in the metropolitan centre; however, they do pay the price of their economic sovereignty with policy decision making chasing corporate interests (Patnaik 2015).

The structure of the new international division of labour shaped in global value chains (GVC) means low value-adding, labour-intensive and environmentally and socially costly operations shift from developed to developing countries. High value-adding capital and technology-intensive operations (including R&D, designing and manufacturing of crucial high-tech components) remain based in developed countries in complete control of metropolitan capital (Pratap 2014b). By monopolistic control on markets, finances and critical technologies, the Transnational Corporations (TNC) of metropolitan capital can exercise effective control of whole value chains and capture the significant share of profits generated across the value chains across the globe.

Moreover, the design of global value chains scatters various stages of production operations across different countries. Accordingly, no country is in a position to impact the value chain in any significant way, so their bargaining power with TNC brands is meagre. Also, no country can master the technology to move up the value chain and create risk by manufacturing competitive brands. GVCs are structured in such a way that moving to higher value chain levels requires a pre-existing global presence, robust technological capabilities and a skilled workforce of significant size and therefore it acts as an effective barrier for firms in developing countries to move up the value chain.

Acquiring technological capabilities has become highly expensive. Equipped and protected by intellectual property rights, the TNCs exercise effective control over technology and are never willing to share it with firms in developing countries. In such situations, many times, to acquire technological capabilities, the only option left is to gain a firm in a developed country. Obviously, this option can be taken up only by very few comparatively large corporations with healthy finances, which is rare in developing countries. Thus, we find that along with brands; most first-tier supplier companies are also from developed countries. The local subcontractors are rare even in the second tier of the supply chain. The majority of the local manufacturing is at the third tier engaging in highly labour-intensive and low value-adding operations.

On the other hand, by their control of the whole value chain, the brand companies create intense competition among various subcontracting firms and apply consistent pressure to minimise costs. Each level of the value chain translates these dynamics as an inbuilt feature of the GVCs. To win in this competition and get the work orders from the brand companies or suppliers at higher levels of the value chain, the subcontracting companies in turn resort to the intensification of labour exploitation by all means possible, to ensure the brands' maximum potential profits and significant profits for themselves. Global value chains thus create a situation in which local industries are locked in low value-added production and labour, in general, is locked in low wages and precarious conditions (Schmitz 2006, p. 558).

The new international division of labour also increases the import bills of developing countries, as the production itself requires the import of various parts from other countries. Additionally, the rosy picture of manufacturing export performance in data is misleading because the local value-added content in those exports is minimal. The typical structure of the GVC production system creates a situation where in the country many times imports products it manufactured. On the other hand, by scrapping or reducing the import duties as required by WTO, the remaining industries face a severe crisis due to the dumping of cheaper foreign goods, ultimately leading to deindustrialisation.

It is worth mentioning here that the import ratio in the manufacturing output in India has been drastically increasing in recent decades. The trade ratio (excluding petroleum, oil and lubricants exports) that was showing a trade surplus till 2003 became a deficit post 2003/04. The deficit further increased in the slowdown (2004–2008), when import competition displaced domestic production to a considerable extent (Mehrotra et al. 2014; Mohanty 2013).

Currently, the primary focus of Make in India is electronics, and even after recording significant expansion, value-added in Indian electronics manufacturing is only 5–10%. In value terms, the sector's imports are second only to the country's oil imports; if this situation continues, by 2020, electronics imports may exceed oil imports (Pratap 2014a). Since 2001 we observe faster growth in the exports of manufactured products that rank high regarding import intensity (Mehrotra et al. 2014). In the Indian manufacturing sector as a whole, the import intensity of exports increased from 12.89% in 1993–94 to 16.77% in 1998–99 and further rose to 29.6% in 2007–08. It is important to note that manufacturing sector constitutes more than 70% of Indian exports (Mahua 2014). Mehrotra has argued that India's domestic manufacturing sector suffer as a result of foreign competition, reducing India to the status of producing intermediate goods and importing finished goods from neighbouring countries (Mehrotra et al. 2014).

Accompanied by rising import intensity is the rising capital intensity of manufacturing. The labour-to-capital ratio in Indian organised manufacturing declined from 0.179 in 2001–02 to 0.165 in 2004–05 and further to 0.087 in 2009–10 and even further to 0.0789 in 2011–12 (Mehrotra et al. 2014). The rising import and capital intensity of manufacturing indicate that the current growth dynamics have a limited capacity to generate any significant employment. Given these situations, as Rodrik argues: 'Technological advances have rendered manufacturing much more skill and capital-intensive than it was in the past, even at the low-quality end of the spectrum. As a result, the capacity of manufacturing to absorb labour has become much more limited. It will be impossible for the next generation of industrialising countries to move 25% or more of their workforce into manufacturing, as East Asian economies did' (Rodrik 2012).

On the one hand, the import intensity of trade and export-based manufacturing reflects a transfer of wealth from India and other developing countries to metropolitan countries. Furthermore, the capital intensity of manufacturing has generated jobless growth. Smith (2012) has argued that when considered in the context of a global value chain, the GDP reflects value captured as opposed to value added, with actors in core imperialist countries controlling the production process to extract maximum value from countries like India.

Moreover, the new international division of labour forces intense competition among developing countries to offer better prospects to global capital to get a higher share of FDI and export orders. Global value chains force similar intense competition among subcontracting firms to offer better profits to get work orders. These dynamics have been disastrous for labour, regarding enforcing large-scale formalisation of the workforce and establishing an anti-labour industrial relations regime. Overall, this has drastically reduced the collective bargaining power of labour and intensified exploitation.

Agrarian Crisis and Its Significance

Recent literature studying agriculture in India has suggested that India's agricultural sector is no longer in crisis. Chand and Parappurath (2012, p. 56) for example, use aggregate growth statistics to argue for a reversal of agricultural fortunes, which leads them to conclude that there has been an "an unambiguous turnaround in the years coinciding with the Eleventh Five-Year Plan (2007–12)". Extending their argument, Chand and Parappurath laud the agricultural performance of BJP led states (pp. 58–9) and suggested that increased private sector involvement is the explanatory cause for the turnaround in agriculture (p61). The political implication of this chapter is that further liberalisation and private sector participation in the agricultural sector would be unambiguously good for the industry.

Ghosh (2016) has argued that this has been the core consensus of Indian governments in the post-liberalisation period. "[L]arge investments by private corporate capital that are expected to deliver both more rapid growth, and more formal employment, and the required diversification out of low-productivity primary activities and petty services. To that end, the many shackles on such capital, in the form of internal and external regulation, were sought to be removed, and also, over time various incentives were provided to encourage more rapid rates of private investment."

In our analysis, it is possible to look at the entirety of agriculture in India and suggest that there is no crisis based on the sector's overall performance as seems to be the consensus in the literature (Ghosh 2016; Ramachandran 2011, p. 56; Lerche 2011, 2013; Chand and Parappurathu 2012). Much in the same way, it is possible to look at India's overall economic performance and discount structural problems associated with poverty and inequality. If we accept the possibility that class stratification exists within the agricultural sector, it becomes possible to consider a crisis of small and marginal farmers within the broader context of a growing and viable economic sector (Lerche 2013, p. 50).

The average size of operational land holdings in India is now at an unsustainable level. From 1970–71 to 2010–11, the average size of operational holdings decreased from 2.28 ha to 1.16 ha. The total number of operational holdings increased from 71 million in 1970–71 to 138 million in 2010–11, swelling the number of marginal (<1 ha) and small (1–2 ha) land holdings by 56 million and 11 million, respectively. The average size of marginal holdings is only 0.38 ha, and they currently constitute 67% of the operational holdings but only 22% of operated areas in 2010–11. The operated zones of small land holdings also increased from 12% to 22% during the same period. Marginal and small land holdings together constitute about 85% of operational holdings and 44% of the operated areas in the country. The shift from subsistence agriculture to a commercial agriculture system and alarmingly rising input costs have made cultivation in small farms mostly unsustainable (National Bank for Agriculture and Rural Development [NABARD] 2014).

Regarding marginal farmers for example, Lerche (2011, p. 106) has demonstrated that "…more than 70 percent of all landowners fall into the category of 'marginal farmers' owning less than one hectare of land, up from 39 percent in 1960–61, while less than 1 percent own more than 10 hectares, down from 5 percent in 1960–61. More than half of the income of marginal farmers is from wages, so this group is best understood as wage workers who receive a subsidiary income from the plots of land that they own." This analysis suggests a polarisation of ownership patterns and a transformation of small and marginal farmers into a semi-proletariat. Ramachandran (2011, p. 62) even argues that it is no longer relevant to separate between agricultural and non-agricultural workers in village settings.

The problem with this is that India's agriculture requires fewer workers especially outside of the harvest season. This falling demand for agricultural labour has "created a pauperised, destitute, permanent reserve army of labour, consisting of men, women and children, primarily but not only from the lowest castes. This is reinforced by the labour regime in the non-agricultural sectors, which is based on formalised, casual or short-term contractual employment with inferior pay and sometimes extremely humiliating conditions of work (Lerche 2011, p. 113)." The introduction of neo-liberal principles of formalised employment within what used to be formal-sector employment exacerbates this.

It was considered a great paradox of the Indian economy that capitalist development was not leading to the disappearance of small farms and small economies in general and the consolidation of land holdings. Chandrasekhar has discussed the assumption behind this (2007, p. 62), arguing that in a relatively closed economy, agricultural productivity acted as a strong constraint limiting the possibilities of economic transformation. Chandrasekhar observes that a critical change occurred in the late 1980s and early 1990s as India began to liberalise its economy, and as the world of global finance began to penetrate (Ibid, p. 66). As a result of this, it became possible for the non-agricultural sector to grow significantly faster than the agricultural sector, in such a way that agriculture was no longer a constraint on India's overall growth. In addition to this, the fact that it was India's services sector (less dependent on agricultural inputs) which grew is a further reason that agricultural growth became decoupled from non-agricultural growth (Ibid, p. 67). The share of agriculture and allied activities in the GDP declined progressively from independence onward from 41.54% in 1951/2 to 12.02% in 2011/12 (Open Government Data Platform India 2016a).

However, agriculture's share in the workforce declined less markedly and still constitutes over half the workforce (Open Government Data Platform India 2016b). Even if the rural population was facing hardship, the industry was not able to offer sufficient sustainable and decent alternative livelihood opportunities. There is a reluctance to part with traditional occupations that at least guaranteed a subsistence minimum. This subsistence level is now coming under sustained pressure. With the increasing input costs and decreasing operational size of landholdings, rural people are forced to migrate at least seasonally for survival; the recurrent droughts have acted as the final blow to force many to move out of agriculture.

The relative recentness of this trend should also be noted, as should its explicit relationship with India's liberalisation. As recently as the 1980s, the GDP growth rate in agriculture was more than 3% per annum. In liberalisation phase, it drastically declined, eventually falling to a low of 1.6% per annum in 2005 (Dev 2014). One notable result of this has been the wave of farmers' suicides in India, which is ongoing. Total farmer suicides in the country from 1995 to 2014 were over 300,000 (Sainath 2015).

Escaping Precarity and Poverty Is Possible: Menda's Lessons

In light of these dark conditions, scholars and activists alike consider whether there is any cause for optimism in the current Indian political scenario. In this section, we consider Menda village's response to the current neoliberal dynamics. We argue that Menda has built a robust social movement as a collective response that has stood in the face of the current developmental dynamics.

As noted previously, Menda is a small tribal village in the Gadchiroli district of Maharashtra, India and is part of Lekha Panchayat (village council), popularly known as Menda Lekha. There are currently 105 families and about 300 voters in the village. The village is about 1900 ha of land, which includes 100 ha of agriculture land and 1800 ha of forest. The Menda people call themselves the Koya (meaning human) tribe; however, they are listed as the Gond tribe probably because their area falls in Gondwana land.

The new awakening in the village began in the late 1970s, when the union government proposed two dams in the Gadchiroli region, presenting the villagers with the imminent threat of displacement (Pathak 2009, p. 392). The villagers joined the protest movement against the construction of dams. These dams were an existential threat, and if implemented, it would have uprooted the tribes from their traditional homes, their cultural roots and their livelihoods. The tribal peoples of the region united on this issue which led a long and vigorous protest. Finally, they won this battle, and the government was compelled to withdraw the proposals of dam projects in 1985 (Ibid).

This mass movement raised the political consciousness of the people and developed visionary leadership in the village. Devaji Tofa, a Menda villager, emerged as the movement's leader during this political awakening. The movement also linked up with visionary social activists in the region committed to working for social reforms. The Gandhian Mohan Hirabhai Hiralal was one such social activist, who became the friend, philosopher and guide of the Menda people's movement for social transformation.

After this movement, Abhyas Gats (study circles) started in the village to conceptualise responses to challenges faced by the village. The expectation existed that all adult men and women would participate. This led to a philosophy of self-government under the slogan of 'Dilli Mumbai Amcha Sarkar, Amache Ganavat Amhich Sarkar', meaning the governments in Delhi and Mumbai (Central government and state government) are our governments, but here in our village, we are the government (Singh 2009). The villagers agreed upon the need to manage all resources collectively to effect any great change in the village. Jungle Bachao Manav Bachao Andolan (Save Forest, Save Humanity Movement) began in 1987, led by Devaji Tofa and Mohan Hirabhai Hiralal (Dhavse 2003; Singh 2009). We can see the movement's focus in the decisions taken in Abhyas Gat for implementation at the village level in Menda (Ibid):

1. The village would meet its requirements from the surrounding forests in a sustainable way without paying any fee to the government.

2. Prohibition of outsiders carrying out forest activities without Gram Sabha permission (which includes one member from every household).
3. Prohibition of commercial exploitation of the forests, except for Non-Timber Forest Produce.
4. Regular forest patrols by villagers.
5. They would regulate the number of resources they could extract from the forests.
6. Water and soil conservation measures would be taken against soil erosion.
7. Villagers would collectively work on firefighting activities.
8. Encroachment would not be allowed.
9. A Vana Suraksha Samiti (VSS) was formed, with at least two members of each household, to implement the discussion above.

These decisions had two dimensions: (a) an assertion of rights of the tribal people over the forest; and (b) the institutionalisation of the Abhyas Gat for making decisions. This constituted a revival of the traditional system of Gram Sabha, which was a kind of declaration that Gram Sabha was a supreme governing institution at the village level. Office bearers of Gram Sabha were unanimously elected, and they gradually collected all legal, revenue and political documents related to the village to empower themselves.

During the same time, the Gram Sabha also decided to construct and revive the Ghotul system. A Ghotul was a traditional education system of tribal people. Later, the formal school system was extended to the tribal areas as well, and schools were opened, but they did not teach the traditional knowledge of the life and culture of the tribal peoples, and so Ghotuls did not lose their relevance. Previously, the forest department had stopped the construction of Ghotuls, as they were made using teakwood, which the department considered state property (Singh 2009). The decision to revive the Ghotul communicated two messages: (a) moving toward the roots, and (b) challenging the authority of forest department and asserting their rights over the forest.

The forest department reacted strongly against this, destroyed the newly erected Ghotul in Menda and seized all the teakwood used to make it. After that, Ghotuls took the form of tribal movement across the region. In a meeting of 32 villages, the various tribal peoples decided to collectively disobey the forest department and construct Ghotuls in every village.

Ghotuls were constructed in 12 villages along with Menda. They collectively declared that they would reconstruct Ghotuls every time the forest department destroyed it. It was not possible for the forest department to enter into this futile battle; thus, they never attempted to destroy the Ghotuls again.

The initial struggles of the Menda people focused on achieving mastery over self, particularly against individualism and alcoholism. Devaji Tofa argued that "Without creating collective dynamics, collective thinking and establishing the priority of collective interest over individual concern, it is hard to move. On the other hand, without getting rid of excessive alcoholism, it is hard to channel the energy of the village toward any significant transformative work (Devaji Tofa, Personal Correspondence, 9 October 2015)." The village leadership explicitly rejected a top-down approach, realising decisions imposed on the people would have no meaning. It took almost five years of discussions, both in Abhyas Gat and through word of mouth, to enlighten the people. Finally, in 1987–88, the Gram Sabha decided unanimously to regulate the use of alcohol through a blanket ban on procuring liquor from the market. The Gram Sabha would also control the production of traditional liquor in the village for ceremonial purposes.

In 1991, the Menda villagers faced another major challenge when the forest department declared Menda forest a reserve forest, an official category of protected forest, wherein forest communities are not allowed to use forest resources (Singh 2009). The forest department responded to their new assertions of sovereignty by challenging their initiatives toward asserting their rights over the forest. The Menda people continued implementing their decisions to protect and manage the forest.

Against the forest department's challenge, Menda Gram Sabha registered as a non-profit organisation in the name of Gaon Niyojan Va Vikas Parishad (a village planning and development organisation) to give legitimacy to their activities. After the forest had been declared a reserve forest, there were incidences of forest officials that were taking bribes from the village people for the use of forest resources. During this period, Menda Gram Sabha made a landmark decision to end corruption. It issued a directive that people must ask for a receipt from government officials for whatever money they paid them and that if anyone who was paying money to the government officials were not able to produce this receipt, the Gram Sabha would charge him/her same amount of money (Singh 2009). This effectively ended the bribing system of forest officials.

Menda Gram Sabha vigorously protested against declaring Menda forest a reserve forest. In the meantime, in 1992, the State of Maharashtra adopted a joint forest management (JFM) resolution, under which degraded forests were to be handed over to villagers for regeneration and managed jointly by the villagers and the forest department (Singh 2009; Pathak 2009). However, forests in Gadchiroli district were rich canopy forests, not degraded forests, meaning Menda would not obtain the benefits of the JFM. The villagers fought hard for this and finally, in 1996, the state government included Menda in the JFM (Singh 2009). After the state government's decision, the right of Menda Gram Sabha to manage the forests was recognised, and it was able to develop and implement its plans to sustainably manage the natural resources in the village revenue area.

Water shortages in 1993 inspired the Gram Sabha to establish a pond in a field with proper drainage. The forest department opposed this, but the villagers claimed that they were merely enlarging and maintaining a forest pond. On the other hand, this work was time-consuming and seemed increasingly impossible to complete voluntarily, as the villagers endured this period without earnings. The Gram Sabha was able to channel some money from the government's Employment Guarantee Fund for the village, but from this, they were able to construct only half of the pond (Singh 2009).

After the monsoon of 1994, half of the pond was full, and the Gram Sabha decided to use it for fish cultivation. The Gram Sabha passed a resolution that those who will help dig the other half of the pond may catch fish in return, enabling completion of the other part of the pond. Fish cultivation continues to be done in this pond and is cleaned annually through the same exchange system. Otherwise, people can also obtain fish by paying money to the Gram Sabha or providing a commensurate amount of labour (Singh 2009). This pond has great significance for the village, as it ensures at least one crop in the surrounding fields.

The Scheduled Tribes and Other Traditional Forest Dwellers (Recognition of Forest Rights) Act was enacted in 2006, and after a long struggle, Menda was able to acquire community rights over the forest in 2009 (Singh 2009). Now the Gram Sabha has legitimate rights to manage its two sq. km of forest. Menda and Marda were the first two villages to get these rights. This is only the part of the story that briefly describes their struggles and achievements mainly regarding asserting and winning the community rights over the forest, which formed the base for various experiments of social transformation.

The New Collectivity

During our interviews, Tofa argued that 'Private property is the leading cause of poverty and all evils. There is no initiative for considering all the natural resources as collective property and no initiative to conserve them, and this is the reason for all the problems. We believe in collective property; tribal people traditionally had common ownership and no private property (Devaji Tofa, Personal Communication, 9 October 2015)'.

Menda Gram Sabha meetings and Abhyas Gats focused on imparting the importance of collective property. Every development in Menda emphasised a collective way of living and working, the ideological consensus around which took years of political work to establish. In the later phase when this consensus evolved, the members of the Gram Sabha systematically started building systems of collectivity. This is particularly notable in the context of the forcefulness of state-led de-collectivisation in China, supposedly heralding the end of collective systems of living and working as an effective means of development (Xu 2013), and the general neoliberal turn, which has characterised the political climate in the past 30 years worldwide. These factors have acted as a catalyst for a general loss of faith in collective systems. Against this backdrop, Menda is part of a broader story associating economic development with collectivism. This can be demonstrated by other fieldwork undertaken by us in Banjari village in Chhattisgarh, along with documented examples in China's Nanjie village (Hou 2013, p. 23), and some villages in Yunnan province (Holden et al. 2011, p. 9).

The Gram Sabha reached consensus and decided that all cattle and bullocks, and farm implements including tractors, even if owned by individual families, would be considered its collective property and any financial assistance needed to improve them would be provided by it.

Fire safety work is done periodically to protect the forest, and it requires a significant number of workers. Fire breaks measuring 20–25 sq. foot areas are cleared in the forest so that fires cannot spread. The Gram Sabha declared that this is the collective and joint responsibility of all families in the village. Therefore, teams were made for this purpose with one person from each household participating in performing unwaged work.

The Gram Sabha also decided to collectivise the water supply and infrastructure. Huge wells planned to be constructed in the village fields would be joint property. If any additional money was needed over and above the government assistance to maintain the water supply, the Gram Sabha fund would be used.

There was a significant change in the way the family system was understood in the village, with the decision that children were the collective responsibility of the village and not the private property of individual households. This made the Gram Sabha, and thereby the entire village, collectively responsible for their education and overall development. If any child wanted to pursue higher education and needed financial assistance, the Gram Sabha pledged to provide aid. In marriages, each family contributed equally to the cost of the wedding, ending the systemic burden on the daughter's family.

Collective herd rearing was established as a practice between 2000 and 2002. Before this, villagers paid an amount to one or two people who cared for the village herd and took them grazing in the forests. This system was abolished in favour of a rotating roster system in which each family took turns managing the herd for a few days each in groups of two to three persons each day.

Most importantly, in 2011, the village people by consensus willingly donated all their land titles to the Gram Sabha, finalising the collectivization of village property. There were discussions in the Gram Sabha on this subject for many years but only after a consensus was reached did this dream become a reality. The dynamics of collective or cooperative farming do not exist yet with households cultivating their fields individually. There are some elements of cooperative farming through commonly owned and managed land, irrigation infrastructure, farming implements and herds. There is no hiring of labour, and everyone helps everyone in need. For example, in harvesting, each household contributes a small part of their harvest to the Gram Sabha to create a grain bank, and anyone in need (e.g. during marriage) can borrow grain and return it later.

The importance of the Gram Sabha owning all land is significant in two other important aspects. Firstly the village became wholly protected, as no individual farmer could sell land or be compelled or bribed to agree for land to be acquired by an industrialisation or urbanisation project. On the other hand, the Gram Sabha assumed the responsibility to help any household in distress. After the land had been donated by all households to the Gram Sabha, Menda Gram Sabha obtained the status of an independent panchayat (village council) for all practical purposes.

Before 2011, Menda Gram Sabha had faced problems in implementing its goals because it was legally part of Lekha Panchayat. On the one hand, all government programs were to be implemented through Lekha Panchayat while on the contrary, the Panchayat sometimes created problems because

Menda was increasingly seeking independent power and Lekha Panchayat wanted to retain control over the village. Menda Gram Sabha used the forgotten Maharashtra Gram Dan Act of 1964, providing that if land-owning farmers in a village donate 75% of their land to the Gram Sabha, then it becomes a Gram Dan Village where the relevant powers of the Gram Panchayat pass on to the Gram Sabha of the Gram Dan Village. So after the Gram Sabha became the legal owner of all land in Menda, it also became an independent panchayat.

The New Democratic System

During our interviews, Tofa argued: 'We believe in selection and not election, i.e. consensus and not majority-minority…Elections based on a majority and minority create a divide among the people and are the cause of many problems (Devaji Tofa, Personal Correspondence, 19 February 2016)'.

In Menda Gram Sabha, all decisions are made by consensus rather than the majority rule. Representatives or office bearers of Menda Gram Sabha and its various committees are elected by consensus. The competitive election process is expensive, and consensus saves these costs and avoids conflicts.

The question of whether a consensus model remains viable beyond the village level remains an open one. In a more homogenous socio-economic and political setting, his theory may work and is worth considering, but it is less clear that this system would work in societies with conflict of interests or ideologies. Nonetheless, this theory has been observed to work well in Menda and yielded outcomes worth celebrating.

The village philosophy is also centred on an idea that there is no need for a permanent group of leaders. Instead, the members of the village panchayat stress a democratic system in which people can collectively decide on issues to the highest possible extent. Committee systems in Menda are based on this conceptualization, as for the coordinators of committees have a limited tenure system where committee members must change every three years. This system attempts to prevent the bureaucratization of the committee process. If any office bearer is proved inefficient or does something wrong, he/she can be replaced any time through a decision made by the Gram Sabha, which manages the day-to-day governance of the village through various committees with responsibilities to carry out and coordinate activities.

Visible Improvements in the People's Lives and Well-Being

> We see the welfare of people regarding accessibility and control over natural resources. To be empowered requires a collective way of living and working that creates happiness in life and all kinds of social security; the people must be empowered to create such collective institutions that help them survive in hard times. (Devaji Tofa, Personal Correspondence, 20 February 2016)

Menda Gram Sabha has been able to bring about a series of positive changes in the socio-politico-economic dynamics of the village through a collective way of living and also working through the sustainable development as well as the use of natural resources to increase employment and earnings.

It is worth noting that Menda Gram Sabha earned about Rs 10 million by selling bamboo in 2011–12. The Gram Sabha currently has Rs 5 million invested in a fixed deposit. It is confident enough for overall improvements in the coming years, and it has declared that it will not accept any grants from any agencies (except government) and will only take loans. Our interviews confirmed that the village as a whole has maintained this practice and has been reluctant to get involved with any NGOs.

The Gram Sabha has been able to generate enough employment in various activities, and this has a visible impact in that there is no distress migration (short-term or long-term) from the village. Education among the children has increased. Now almost all children go to school with some obtaining higher education. Currently, 12 youth in the village are educated up to the 12th standard, and 4 are university graduates who work and lives in the village. As the variety and complexity of activities undertaken by the Gram Sabha increases, these skills are needed in the village, which is why it has been willing to support the children to pursue higher education.

Conclusion

India is a country with a massive, historically created labour surplus typically overcrowding the agriculture sector. The specific conditions of India's capitalist development have prevented the generation of meaningful employment and the easing of the burden of surplus labour from agriculture.

Overall job growth in India is dismal and restricted mainly to non-agriculture and non-manufacturing sectors. There is a visible shift in the workforce from agriculture to urban sectors. However, rather than any positive development, this reflects a systemic crisis of farming. This is why a large part of this additional employment emerges as casual labour in non-manufacturing industries, the result of which is a general downfall in real wages and the labour share of the GDP.

In such situations, this crisis can be resolved only by extensive land reforms. This would necessitate the equitable distribution of land and other occupational natural resources. It would also require collective integration of land holdings to create economies of scale through collective or cooperative farming. Also, it would be necessary to reverse the current policies on agriculture. Meaning, nationalise or de-monopolize and de-corporatize agricultural inputs, strictly regulate the prices of primary commodities and remove infrastructural constraints for agriculture.

This may increase the decent livelihood opportunities in the agricultural sector and other natural resource-based traditional sectors and efficiently reduce the overall rate of unemployment and poverty. This may significantly increase the rural population's purchasing power and develop an effective market for industrial goods, thereby accelerating industrial growth that may, in turn, further accelerate agriculture growth precisely by way of offering more decent employment opportunities and reducing the load of the surplus population on agriculture. This may be the best possible alternative from the people's perspective.

From this point of view, the people's initiative for socio-economic transformation in Menda village of Maharashtra gains immense significance. By way of building a new collectivity with new democratic dynamics, the Gram Sabha was, from its inception until the present day, able to channel the mental and physical energies of the village toward the socio-economic transformation of village life. They were able to regenerate and develop natural resources, increase irrigation facilities, increase employment and income, develop social cohesion and improve living standards.

Their achievements are most powerfully reflected in multiple critical parameters. Distress migration completely stopped from the village. About 60% of children study up to senior secondary standards, and some are pursuing higher education. The grain bank and village funds are sufficient enough to provide security in times of distress. Water resources are regenerated, and work is going on to develop more substantial irrigation infrastructures. New democratic systems have developed greater social cohesion that is reflected in the Gram Dan (all households donating their land titles to the Gram Sabha).

This, in turn, provides excellent opportunities for moving toward some cooperative farming. From selling simple forest produce, now they are moving toward manufacturing products like bamboo crafts and the processing of honey. Biogas plants linked with toilets have both resolved the problems of waste and dependence on forests for firewood also producing organic manure for agriculture and reducing input costs. The Gram Sabha is now planning to build a fertiliser manufacturing plant in the village that will further lower the cost of inputs, which may also increase the employment and earnings of the village people.

A large part of rural India is facing a similar situation as Menda, and its success story offers an effective strategy for helping people to transform their realities and move out of precarity and poverty. This may also accelerate India's overall economic development. Menda's collectivization example provides an essential counterweight to arguments that have been made against collective institutions and property since the advent of neoliberalism.

References

Agrawal, Pradeep. 2015. *Reducing poverty in India: The role of economic growth. IEG Working Paper No. 349.* Available from: http://www.iegindia.org/upload/publication/Workpap/wp349.pdf

Biel, Robert. 2015. *Eurocentrism and the communist movement.* Kersplebedeb: Montreal.

Chand, Ramesh and Parappurath, Shinoj. 2012. Temporal and Spatial Variations in Agricultural Growth and its Determinants. *Economic and Political Weekly.* Vol 47, No 26

Chandrasekhar, CP. 2007. The Progress of "Reform" and the Retrogression of Agriculture. *Social Scientist.* Vol 35, No 1–2.

CPI (Maoist). 2004. *Strategy and tactics of the Indian revolution.* Available from: http://www.bannedthought.net/India/CPI-Maoist-Docs/Founding/StrategyTactics-pamphlet.pdf

Dai, Yannian. 1987. An important thesis on building socialism. *Beijing Review* Vol 30, no. 45.

Das, Raju. 2010. Radical peasant movements and rural distress in India. In: *India's new economic policy: A critical analysis.* Waquar Ahmed and Amitabh Kundu. Routledge: London.

De Haan, Arjan and Thorat, Sukhadeo. 2013. *Inclusive growth: More than safety nets. SIG Working Paper 2013/1.* Available from: https://www.idrc.ca/sites/default/files/sp/Documents%20EN/SIG_WP13-1_InclGrowth.pdf

Dhavse, Rasika. 2003. *The Transformation of Mendha-Lekha.* Available from: http://indiatogether.org/mendha-government

Ghosh, Jayati. 2016. Reaping Distress. *Frontline.* August 5. Available from: http://www.frontline.in/cover-story/reaping-distress/article8870098.ece

Holden, S.T, Xu, J. and Jiang, X. 2011. Collective versus individual property: Tenure security and forest tenure reforms in China. Available from: https://brage.bibsys.no/xmlui/bitstream/handle/11250/2477955/CLTS_WP4_2011.pdf?sequence=1&isAllowed=y

Hou, X. 2013. *Community capitalism in China: The state, the market, and collectivism.* Cambridge: Cambridge University Press.

Karat, P. 2007. 'Double-speak' charge: maligning the CPI(M). *People's Democracy* 31, no. 4. Available from: http://pd.cpim.org/2007/0128/01282007_prakash.htm

Kerswell, Timothy. 2015. Samir Amin. In: *The Encyclopedia of Imperialism and Anti-Imperialism*, Ness, Immanuel and Cope, Zak, eds., 5–9 Palgrave: Basingstoke.

Lerche, Jens. 2011. Agrarian Crisis and Agrarian Questions in India. *Journal of Agrarian Change.* Vol 11, No 1.

Lerche, Jens. 2013. The Agrarian Question in Neo-liberal India: Agrarian Transition Bypassed? *Journal of Agrarian Change.* Vol 13, No 3.

Lewis, W.A. 1954. Economic development with unlimited supplies of labor. *The Manchester School.* Vol 22, no. 2: 139–91.

Mahua, Paul. 2014. *Import intensity and its impact on exports, output and employment; Working Paper-167.* Institute for Studies in Industrial Development: New Delhi http://www.isid.org.in/pdf/WP167.pdf

Make in India. 2016. *Smart cities.* Available from: http://www.makeinindia.com/article/-/v/internet-of-things

Marx, K. and Engels, F. 1975. *Collected works* (CW6). Progress Publishers: Moscow.

McCarthy, Greg. 1985. The socialist transition and the socialist mode of production. In: *Chinese Marxism in flux 1978–84: Essays on epistemology, ideology and political economy*, ed. Bill Brugger, 142–171, London: Croom Helm.

Mehrotra, Santosh, Sinha, Sharmistha, Parida, Jajati and Gandhi, Ankita. 2014. *Why a jobs turnaround despite Slowing growth?* Occasional Papers, Institute of Applied Manpower Research, Planning Commission, Government of India.

Mohanty, M. 2013. *Growth and globalization: An anatomy of the slowdown of the Indian economy.* Presented at the Indian Institute of Management, Calcutta March 2013.

NABARD. 2014. Agricultural land holdings pattern in India; *NABARD Rural Pulse* I: Jan.–Feb. 2014; https://www.nabard.org/Publication/Rural_Pulse_final142014.pdf

Open Government Data Platform India. 2016a. *GDP of India and major sectors of economy, share of each sector to GDP and growth rate of GDP and other sectors of economy 1951–52 onward.* Available from: https://data.gov.in/catalog/gdp-india-and-major-sectors-economy-share-each-sector-gdp-and-growth-rate-gdp-and-other

Open Government Data Platform India. 2016b. *Proportionate share of sectors in employment (in percentage).* Available from: https://data.gov.in/catalog/proportionate-share-sectors-employment-percentage

Sainath, P. 2015. *The slaughter of suicide data.* Available from: https://psainath.org/the-slaughter-of-suicide-data/

Pathak, Neema (Ed). 2009. *Community Conserved Areas in India: A Directory.* Pune: Kalpavriksh.

Patnaik, Prabhat. 2009. A perspective on the growth process in India and China. Available from: www.networkideas.org/working/jun2009/05_2009.pdf

Patnaik, Prabhat. 2011. The myths of capitalism. *People's Democracy*, 3rd July 2011; http://pd.cpim.org/2011/0703_pd/07032011_7.html

Patnaik, Prabhat. 2015. The slogan of 'Make in India'. *People's Democracy* XXXIX, no. 44, November 8, 2015; http://www.macroscan.org/cur/nov15/pdf/Make_India.pdf

Planning Commission: Government of India. 2008. *Eleventh five-year plan 2007–2012.* Oxford University Press: New Delhi.

Pratap, Surendra. 2014a. *Workers in the supply chain of electronics industry in India, in the book, Labour Rights in High-tech Electronics.* Hong Kong: AMRC.

Pratap, Surendra. 2014b. Emerging trends in factory Asia: International capital mobility, global value chains and the labor movements; AMRC, Hong Kong.

Ramachandran, VK. 2011. The State of Agrarian Relations in India Today. *The Marxist.* Vol 37, No 1–2.

Rodrik, Dani. 2012. *No more growth miracles.* Available from: http://www.project-syndicate.org/commentary/no-more-growth-miracles-by-dani-rodrik

Rostow, W. 1960. *The stages of economic growth: A non-communist manifesto.* London: Cambridge University Press.

Dev, S Mahendra. 2014. *Small farmers in India: Challenges and opportunities.* WP-2012-014; Indira Gandhi Institute of Development Research, Mumbai, http://www.igidr.ac.in/pdf/publication/WP-2012-014.pdf

Sanyal, S. 2008. *The Indian Renaissance: India's rise after a thousand years of decline.* New Delhi: Penguin (India).

Schmitz, H. 2006. Learning and earning in global garment and footwear chains. *The European Journal of Development Research,* 18, no. 4.

Singh, Supriya. 2009. *Participatory Forest Management in Mendha Lekha, India.* Available from: http://www.ceecec.net/wp-content/uploads/2009/10/Mendha-Lekha-Using-Self-Governance1.pdf

Smith, John. 2012. The GDP Illusion. *Monthly Review* 64, no. 3.

Sun, Yat. 1995. *The Chinese reassessment of socialism: 1976–1992.* Princeton University Press: New Jersey.

UNCTAD. 2012. *Trade and Development Report 2011–12.* United Nations, Geneva.

Xu, Zhun. 2013. The Political Economy of Decollectivization in China. *Monthly Review* Vol 65, Iss 1.

CHAPTER 7

Conclusion: Learning the Lessons

At present, there is a significant ideological campaign by imperialist forces such as the United States, the World Bank and the IMF to press cooperatives into the service of neoliberal ends. This argument is furthered by organisations such as the ILO and the International Cooperatives Alliance which are arguing both for the formation of cooperatives, for their depoliticization and the depoliticization of the trade union movement in general.

Closely linked to this argument is the totalizing discourse of the "informal sector" and the linked argument that the informal sector is a permanent feature of the economy in India and indeed in other countries in the global South. We have argued that India has various groups of workers in vulnerable positions. However, these are by no means inevitable or permanent but rather are products of India's history and political economy. Accordingly, these conditions can be changed through the mobilization of resources in favour of the working class.

We have argued that building cooperatives and other collective ways of living and working are one such possibility, a step on the road beyond capitalism. Additionally, we have argued that such collective methods should be established during capitalism, as opposed to waiting for a post-revolutionary situation. We feel that many of the examples we have analysed in this book show that cooperatives can offer a lot to transformative politics. The examples we considered achieved relative degrees of success, despite relative isolation and a lack of political support. A proactive and transformative approach

T. Kerswell, S. Pratap, *Worker Cooperatives in India*,
https://doi.org/10.1007/978-981-13-0384-5_7

to the building of collective ways of working and living should thus be explored. This should be done keeping in mind the historical lessons of previous collective experiences such as those discussed in this book.

This book has highlighted the experiences of collective or cooperative ways of living and working in India which have been operated or influenced to a significant extent by trade unions or other progressive political forces. The most valuable aspect of the research undertaken on trade union cooperatives in India is to learn the lessons of previous social experiments and use them to inform future strategies in the working class movement.

A critical factor in the success of cooperatives as agents for strengthening the position of the working class is the extent to which they can exert some form of control over the terrain of struggle. The importance of this can be seen in each of the examples which have been presented. In the case of CMSS, the Union retained control over the cooperative societies but did not have control over the mines themselves as a result of the nationalisation of coal. This meant the union was dependent on the state for support and when the state was no longer a willing partner, the movement began to struggle.

Similarly, the Alcond workers cooperative rose to success in no small part due to the existence of a friendly government in the Communist Party of India (Marxist) led Left Front which the union was affiliated. While the Left Front was in power, the workers retained some degree of control over the terrain of struggle due to the ability to source guaranteed supply contracts and friendly terms of business backed by the power of the Left Front state government. The importance of this was highlighted with the very sudden collapse experienced by Alcond when the Trinamool Congress took over in West Bengal and used various bureaucratic methods to undermine the cooperative's position.

Regarding the SEWA Rachaita cooperative, it exists within one of the most saturated, precarious and low paid industries in India, namely the construction sector. SEWA Rachaita has few points of leverage with which to improve the position of its workers, a fact which is compounded by an approach that attempts to rebrand precarious workers as entrepreneurs. When SEWA workers earn at or below the market rates of pay, the claims of SEWA as an organization of empowerment are shown to be dubious.

SEWA's cooperative demonstrates the need for workers struggles to be transformative, building power rather than merely attempting to pursue economic ends within a capitalistic labour market. This is particularly the case when the dynamics of the labour market are so heavily skewed against precarious labour. The massive amount of surplus labour exiting India's rural sector and entering the urban informal sector is disproportionately being absorbed into the construction industry, generating a hard limit around the progress which can be made in the industry without transformative goals.

This highlights the importance of the Menda Lekha example. With rising input costs of agriculture driving small and marginal farmers in India to distress migration, Menda village responded by generating an economy of scale through cooperative ownership and farming. The Menda example highlights a way that workers can circumvent the economic forces compelling them to migrate to precarious industries in the urban informal sector, generating a sustainable livelihood and reducing the size of the reserve army of labour in India's cities.

The second lesson relates to the ideological perspective of the cooperatives. Worker cooperatives are somewhat romanticised by people with a left-wing political persuasion, especially as an alternative to capitalism. Our examples should give cause for why not all cooperatives are equal, and why a healthy degree of skepticism should greet cooperative formation when it is not based on a firm ideological footing.

While this is perhaps not the space to intervene deeply into the various debates within left politics in India, the examples we presented do raise some questions which are worth asking for the sake of the broader trade union and working-class movement.

Firstly, there is a question of relative isolation within the broader Indian political scene and the impact this can have on the cooperative formation. In both the CMSS case and the Alcond case, the political movements were limited by the inability of the respective parties to expand their political influence beyond a localised scene.

CMSS was a highly successful movement in Dalli-Rajhara for a significant period, but it faced problems expanding to other parts of Chhattisgarh, in part because of an inability to channel its successful practice into an advance in theory. Its failure to widen its support base meant that the correlation of forces was not in its favour when struggling with the Indian state.

In the Alcond case, CITU mostly expected and depended upon Left Front support as an affiliated organisation of CPIM. In exchange for this aid, they provided the products of their labour and in doing so helped contribute to the limitation of costs and the development of the state power infrastructure of West Bengal. Despite this, the cooperative workers admitted that apart from the provision of government contracts, and a friendly credit regime, for the Alcond factory, CPIM demonstrated an ambivalent attitude toward the cooperatives largely seeing them in instrumental terms as a way to keep an industrial base in West Bengal.

Alcond's dependence on the Left Front government being in power was highlighted when the Left Front lost government in West Bengal, and Alcond immediately faced a crisis of survival. This raises further questions about the viability of the CPIM's political strategy which has historically placed lots of emphasis on participating in constitutional government, particularly at a state level where it has enjoyed a relative degree of success in some states.

Of most significant concern, however, was SEWA's Rachaita construction cooperative and indeed the SEWA model in general. SEWA's connection to some overseas organisations shows that trade union imperialism has significantly penetrated the organization. The role that SEWA plays is to split and deradicalize the working class movement and to provide ideological cover for the expansion of capitalistic labour relations in India while weakening trade union militancy.

With SEWA expanding its operations to other countries in the global South, as well as in the ITUC, this trend is of immense concern for the global working class movement. SEWA's example demonstrates that trade union imperialism is not a legacy of the Cold War, but rather an ongoing attempt to influence labour politics in the global South and more needs to be done to highlight the role of imperialist governments and imperialist labour movements and their impact.

Menda Lekha's village cooperative is a special case in this regard as it is mostly a primary production cooperative in the agricultural sector. This gives it a relative degree of autonomy as it has the option of structuring production for subsistence rather than for profit if necessary. This gives Menda village significant control over the economic and political terrain within which its movement operates.

The next important factor in the success of the cooperatives is the existence of democracy within the cooperatives themselves. The rise of the CMSS and Alcond cooperatives was in no small part due to the democratisation of the work environment, and the political decision-making process. It is notable that, in the case of CMSS, the more centralised the power structure became, the more ossified its thinking became and the less it was able to respond to the challenges that it faced. As a result of its increasing centralization, Niyogi became an easy target for those with ill intentions for the CMSS movement, and the success of the decapitation strategy employed by capital speaks further to its weakness.

In the case of SEWA, while a formal theoretical level of democracy within the organisation exists, the practical reality is somewhat different. SEWA organisers exploit the legitimacy of their organisation, and the massive differences in power between highly educated and institutionally supported activists, and mostly poor and illiterate workers. This has led to the formation of a top-down decision making culture and the imposition of workplace discipline.

On the other hand, the Menda Lekha cooperative demonstrates the importance of structural democracy and political solidarity in forming sustainable cooperative enterprises. The development of a consensus model of decision making within Menda village is a significant achievement. Further to this, the villagers' identification that votes can be bought led them to develop a unique strategy. By collectivising ownership of the village land, this created a significant obstacle to the divide and rule strategies which have been deployed elsewhere in India where land acquisition has been sought.

The examples provided in this book also demonstrate the importance of the generation of economies of scale, and of mutually supporting interests within the cooperative movement. On the one hand, an organisation like Alcond was relatively isolated economically, depending on the private economy for its inputs and for credit to run its operations. This gave it a critical weakness when, at the behest of the Trinamool Congress government, the banks refused Alcond loans for its working capital.

On the other hand, despite its other limitations, the SEWA organisation can expand its reach, in part because of a vast umbrella of supporting institutions such as SEWA Bank and various other service provision arms. Similarly, Menda village has been able to pool various resources both monetary and land/forest based, and created a system of mutually supporting enterprises.

Sitting somewhat between this is the example of CMSS. During its height, CMSS could be seen actively creating a network of supporting cooperative enterprises. This started with the mining sector but then expanded to include the Shaheed Hospital, cooperative garages, cooperative farming in surrounding villages, and cooperative schooling systems. Its reversal of fortunes has seen these institutions isolated, and yet in their isolation, many of these establishments such as the schools and hospitals, have a lasting impact on the lives of working people in Chhattisgarh.

In conclusion, we feel that this book demonstrates the importance of building collective institutions for workers and that this struggle can, and indeed must, begin within capitalism itself. Having said that, it is essential to consider the ideological moorings of the cooperative movement as these significantly determine not only the individual impact that a collective institution will have on the lives of working-class people but also the broader potential to expand and have a positive influence on the working class as a whole. While many of the cases we considered in this book are social experiments which for various reasons appear to be coming to an end, it is crucial that these examples be celebrated for the successes they achieved and built upon in the future.

Index[1]

[1] Note: Page numbers followed by 'n' refer to notes.

T. Kerswell, S. Pratap, *Worker Cooperatives in India*,
https://doi.org/10.1007/978-981-13-0384-5

The manufacturer's authorised representative in the EU is Springer Nature Customer Service Centre GmbH, Europaplatz 3, 69115 Heidelberg, Germany. If you have any concerns regarding our products, please contact ProductSafety@springernature.com

Printed and bound by CPI Group (UK) Ltd, Croydon, CR0 4YY

25/09/2026

02222897-0017